Practical Parenting

Successful strategies for solving your child's behaviour problems

Glen Stenhouse

Melbourne
OXFORD UNIVERSITY PRESS
Oxford Auckland New York

OXFORD UNIVERSITY PRESS NEW ZEALAND

Oxford New York
Athens Auckland Bangkok Bombay
Calcutta Cape Town Dar es Salaam Delhi
Florence Hong Kong Istanbul Karachi
Kuala Lumpur Madras Madrid Melbourne
Mexico City Nairobi Paris Singapore
Taipei Tokyo Toronto

and associated companies in
Berlin Ibadan

OXFORD is a trade mark of Oxford University Press

© Glen Stenhouse 1996
First published 1996

All rights reserved. No part of this publication may
be reproduced, stored in a retrieval system, or
transmitted, in any form or by any means, without
the prior permission in writing of Oxford University
Press. Within New Zealand, exceptions are allowed
in respect of any fair dealing for the purpose of
research or private study, or criticism or review, as
permitted under the Copyright Act 1962, or in the
case of reprographic reproduction in accordance
with the terms of the licences issued by Copyright
Licensing Limited. Enquiries concerning
reproduction outside these terms and in other
countries should be sent to the Rights Department,
Oxford University Press, at the address below.

Edited by Jo McMillan
Text designed by Steve Randles
Cover design by Steve Randles
Typeset by Scriptorium Desktop Publishing Pty Ltd
Printed by McPherson's Printing Group, Australia
Published by Oxford University Press,
540 Great South Road, Greenlane, PO Box 11-149,
Auckland, New Zealand

Contents

Introduction		1
Part I	**The early years**	
	1 Bonding	4
	2 Encouraging development	9
	3 Toilet training	19
Part II	**Problems at night**	
	4 Night waking	26
	5 Nightmares	35
	6 Bedwetting	43
Part III	**Behaviour management**	
	7 Toddler terrorism	56
	8 Time-out	65
	9 Smacking	69
Part IV	**Conflict**	
	10 Aggression and anger	76
	11 Sibling rivalry	82
Part V	**Born not made**	
	12 Temperament and talent	90
	13 Hyperactivity	95
	14 Specific learning disability	111
Part VI	**Gender and sexuality**	
	15 Girls and boys	120
	16 Sexual behaviour	124

Part VII Relationships and communication
        17 Television   133
        18 Communication   138
        19 When parents separate   148
        20 Self-esteem   154

Where to go for help   162

Index   165

Introduction

Parenting is a job. A hard job. It requires considerable dedication, stamina, energy, perseverance, and patience. It also requires a high degree of knowledge and skill, with no pre-service training. The hours and pay are terrible. And that's the good news.

The bad news is that on top of all of this you will sometimes have to deal with quite serious problems and issues, but will be unsure what to do, or which way to go. That's where this book comes in.

It contains practical suggestions on some of the major behavioural problems that can cause headaches and heartache for parents. These include night waking, bedwetting, toddler terrorism, aggression, sibling rivalry, hyperactivity, and specific learning disability.

It also discusses some common areas in which parents have to think long and hard about how to act, or which direction to take in their parenting. These include encouraging intellectual development, choosing appropriate discipline, monitoring the effects of television, understanding and guiding sexual behaviour, nurturing self-esteem, and minimising the effects of separation on children.

The advice I offer is based on fifteen years' experience as a child psychologist, dealing with almost every difficulty, disability and disorder that can cause distress and worry for parents and children. My suggestions are based on observation of what works, and what doesn't. The opinions I express are also founded on my own experience as a parent, but are, of necessity, filtered through my own personality and values.

Most of the chapters were originally written as articles for the parenting magazine *Little Treasures*, or for the *Treasures Baby Book*, and have been extended or adapted to suit this present format. The chapters are grouped into sections based on common themes, which are also roughly chronological in terms of children's development.

Finally, I always stress that there is no such thing as the perfect parent. The purpose of this book is to help you, not to make you feel guilty about what you do or don't do as a mother or father. There is a very wide margin of error in successful parenting. Children are remarkably accepting, adaptable, and resilient — as long as they always know they are loved.

PART ONE
The Early Years

1 Bonding

Over the last few generations, an army of professionals has been providing truckloads of information and advice for parents on every aspect of bringing up children. Because some of this advice has been conflicting, many parents have become confused and anxious about things that shouldn't be problems at all. A good example of this is fashionably known as 'bonding'.

Bonding refers to the development of a special attachment between parent and child. It is a rather clinical term, like something out of a textbook, and my preference is for the simple, old-fashioned, and much more human word, 'love'. Love between a parent and a child is taken for granted, but where does this powerful emotion come from, and how does it develop?

Evolution

As with many basic human behaviours, the answer probably lies in evolution. The protection given by an adult is essential to a baby's survival, and it is likely that human beings have, through evolution, developed an in-built programme causing adults to respond to a baby's features and behaviour in a protective and caring way. These features include the shape of the baby's face, the kind of movements it makes, and — most certainly — its cry.

A baby's cry is hard to ignore. It makes us feel uncomfortable until we have responded to it and met the baby's need. Crying is a behaviour that is designed to ensure survival: the baby sends a powerful distress signal, and we are wired to respond.

The same is true of toddlers and young children. Their physical appearance, and many of the things they do and say, are very appealing to adults. Small children draw us to them — their 'cuteness' provokes in us a strong desire to be with them, to care for them. This can often be felt not only by the child's parents, but even by strangers, which is an indication of the strength of the signals a young child transmits, signals that say 'look after me'.

Developing a bond

We may be programmed to respond to a baby's helplessness, but parents usually develop a warm and intense bond with their baby that goes far beyond simply meeting its basic physical needs. We enjoy holding the baby, caressing it, talking to it, looking at it, and just being with it. We rearrange our lives to give it all the care and attention we can manage, and even put up with broken sleep for months (sometimes years) on end!

For some parents, this sense of loving attachment is present from the moment of birth; for others, it can take a little while to develop. Regardless of this, the key element in the growth of attachment is *interaction*. Nature has primed us up to be ready to fall in love with our baby, but a deep and lasting bond can only be created by interacting with her.

In recent years there has been a lot of emphasis placed on mothers having immediate, skin-to-skin contact with their babies as soon as they are born. While touching and holding the baby straight after birth is certainly a positive thing to do, that alone cannot create a magical, instantaneous bond. A true bond develops over days, weeks and months as parents get to know their baby as an individual.

It becomes even stronger once the baby is able to respond in some ways to the parents' attentions — the first smile is an excellent example of this. I remember one father telling me that his newborn had caused several weeks of little sleep and total disruption in their lives. He had been ready to take it back to the maternity hospital — until it smiled! All was forgiven. This was the beginning of a real relationship between father and child because the baby was now responding to him. Genuine interaction between parent and baby — parent attends to baby, baby responds to parent — intensifies the feelings of love and caring, because parents can see that their love is now being returned.

Love can take time

Some parents find it hard to love their newborn baby, who sleeps most of the time and generally pays no attention to them. They may feel guilty because they don't feel the expected outpouring of emotion when they first hold their baby. There may be no sense of 'love at first sight'. In fact, this is a quite natural response for some parents, who find that their love grows gradually over weeks and months. Don't worry if there are no warm, fuzzy feelings for that tiny, red-faced, wailing bundle who won't let you sleep, especially if she's your first child.

There are so many things to learn about, worry about, and adjust to in those first weeks that feelings of love may have to take a back seat for a while. The first few months can be plain hard work, and you may simply be too tired to feel like the parents in the magazine advertisements, bathed in a golden glow as they gaze lovingly at their smiling babies. For some mothers, postnatal depression can make it almost impossible to respond to their baby's needs in the way they had hoped and expected to.

Also, some babies are just harder to love than others. Some are very cuddly, and nestle snugly and easily into your arms. Others are not. They seem to resist being cuddled, feel somehow stiff and awkward when you hold them, and wriggle to escape. Some babies have easy, placid temperaments, while others seem to be constantly fussy and irritable. A placid little snuggler is probably going to be easier to love than a non-cuddly fusspot.

Non-cuddly children may well grow up to be non-cuddly adults — and parents. If you are a person who finds it difficult to show physical affection, don't worry. Your baby will get lots of physical contact with you through everyday activities such as feeding, bathing and dressing. As she gets older, you can show your love through smiles, words, as much physical contact as you feel comfortable with, and, most importantly, by spending time with her. The love you feel will shine through in everything you do, even if kisses and cuddles are limited.

Showing your love

But no matter how you show it, it is very important that your child knows she is loved. A sense of being loved and valued unconditionally is essential for your child's sense of security and trust in the world, and it forms the foundation of her self-esteem. An unstable foundation means that she will be unlikely to develop a secure sense of self-worth as she grows.

At the most basic level, we show love for our children through caring for their physical needs, which takes up a large of part of our days and nights when they are babies and toddlers. As they grow, we show our love by creating an environment that is safe, secure and predictable. We also show it by helping them to learn new skills, by supporting and encouraging them in every way along the road to independence.

Words are important too, and as children grow older they need to hear frequently from both parents those three magic little words: 'I love you'. Hugs and cuddles are the icing on the cake.

Bonding, attachment, love — call it what you like — it is a two-way process between parent and child that begins in babyhood, and grows stronger with the passing years. It's what parenting is all about.

Parenting points

- Evolution seems to have programmed adult human beings to respond to a baby's features and behaviour in a protective and caring way.
- There is no magical 'critical period' in which a bond must form between parent and child. Don't worry if there is no sense of 'love at first sight' — it will come.
- The hard work of looking after a baby — particularly a demanding, irritable one — can sometimes drive out feelings of love and affection. This a normal part of real-life parenting.
- Postnatal depression can make it almost impossible to respond to your baby as you had hoped and expected. If you are feeling persistently tearful, sad, and tired, or you feel that you just can't cope with looking after your baby, talk to your doctor.
- Remember, love is more than hugs and kisses. It is shown in everything we do to help our children grow and develop.

2 Encouraging development

What can we do as parents to ensure that our children reach the maximum level of development of which they are capable?

Hot-housing

Most parents today are aware of the benefits of stimulation for early development. They enjoy exposing their toddlers and preschoolers to a wide range of learning experiences and activities, including swimming, playgroup, preschool, gym, dance, and music.

Some parents take this process even further, actively seeking to accelerate their child's development through direct and intensive tuition in specific areas. This approach is based on the belief that exceptional talent is made, not born, and that just about any child can be turned into an Einstein or Mozart, providing his parents are prepared to work hard enough at shaping his development.

The process of making 'superkids' is sometimes called 'hot-housing', which is a very good description of what the theory is all about. The term implies that just as exotic blooms or record-breaking tomatoes can be created through artificially enriched cultivation, so can outstandingly talented children. But can they? Supporters of hot-housing hold an extreme position in the 'nature versus nurture' debate. They are very optimistic in the sense that they believe that every newborn baby is capable of reaching levels of achievement that are usually thought to be attainable by only a few. They see normal developmental milestones as arbitrary barriers to growth, which can be pushed aside by parents who are determined to accelerate their child's development through intensive tuition. They are saying, in fact, that the developing human brain is capable of acquiring information and skills as fast as parents can pour them in, and the earlier the better. But just how does this theory square with what we know about the way in which a child's brain develops?

Brain growth

It is often said that parents should be teaching children a range of subjects from a very early age 'because that's when their brain is developing'. It is true that the brain goes through its most rapid growth before birth and for the first two years of life, by which time it has reached about 75 per cent of its adult size, but this is the very reason why babies and toddlers are not able to absorb complex learning. It is currently thought that the billions of nerve cells (neurons) in the brain are in place well before a child's first birthday, but it is not just the number of neurons that is important. Each neuron forms branch-like connections with surrounding cells, and the complexity of these connections increases as a child grows. It is this increasingly intricate network of links between the neurons, together with other physical changes around the cells, which enables the child to perform gradually more demanding tasks. In other words, there has to be a certain level of nerve-cell development before a child is able to cope with complex behaviours such as walking, speaking and reading. The belief that very young children can be taught almost anything ignores some basic facts about the way in which the brain works.

Language development

The development of children's language is a good example. The growth of language is closely tied to a child's overall perception and understanding of his world. Trying to teach a young child concepts and language structures that are too far in advance of his current level will meet with failure. For example, if children are at the stage of using two-word phrases it is a waste of time trying to teach them to use complete sentences. They will not even be able to imitate more complex language structures successfully, much less retain them or use them spontaneously in their own speech. This is because the development of speech is not simply a process of copying adult models — it is linked to and limited by the child's overall intellectual growth.

The same argument applies to trying to teach toddlers to read. Reading is an extremely complex intellectual task. It does not just involve the ability to recognise a particular group of symbols and make the appropriate noise. That would be a bit like saying that a circus horse that taps its hoof the correct number of times in response to its trainer's signals is capable of doing maths. Reading requires levels of experience, understanding, and language that most children only begin to reach sometime in their fifth year.

Most parents recognise the value of reading to children from an early age, but beginning to teach preschoolers to read and write in a formal and systematic way should be prompted by signs from the children that they are interested in learning. Some children do show early indications of fascination with the printed word, and this can certainly be nurtured, but the lead should always come from the child.

If you feel that your child shows precocious ability in areas such as reading, writing, or maths, seek the advice of a school psychologist or a preschool that emphasises the teaching of pre-academic skills. Preschools vary in philosophy and approach. Some stress the importance of free play and discourage the direct teaching of literacy and numeracy skills. Others encourage more guided, structured play and the exposure of children to early literacy experiences.

Preschoolers should not be hurried to become literate because in the first five years they have so much to learn about the world through direct rather than symbolic experience. There is no doubt, however, that some children are interested in print and number from an early age, and such children should be given the opportunity to explore these areas with professional guidance.

Gifted children

It's a fact, of course, that some children do show amazing abilities very early in life. I have come across many preschoolers with special talents, some who were able to read fluently, others who could draw like ten-year-olds, some who had advanced maths skills, and others who showed the intellectual maturity of much older children. Without exception these children had received very little direct tuition from their parents, who came to me puzzled and sometimes even a little embarrassed by the extraordinary skills of their offspring. Children like this have traditionally been called 'gifted' because their inexplicable talents have seemed like a gift from an unknown source.

Children with special abilities will usually demonstrate early signs of their talent by showing a strong interest in a particular kind of activity, such as reading, music, construction toys, ball games, or drawing. They absorb information in their area of interest very quickly, will spend long periods of time immersed in total concentration, and pick up new skills with little apparent effort. It is usually only after parents have noticed these indications of their child's special ability that they begin to offer him opportunities and encouragement to practise and develop his talent, and perhaps seek advice about how best to nurture it.

In other words, it is almost invariably the case with gifted children that natural aptitude comes first, then recognition of it by parents, followed sometimes by special learning opportunities that help the child to develop his talent further. In my experience, exceptional skills in a particular field (with the possible exception of music), or overall intellectual ability, are never the product solely of intensive tuition or training. Without some degree of innate potential to work with, high-pressure coaching of children is likely to be unproductive in the long run.

Can we do more?

If the concept of hot-housing implies that any child can be turned into a fluent reader by the age of three, a maths whiz by four, or an all-round high IQ genius by five, then it is a mistaken and potentially misleading belief. It ignores the basic biological necessity for the brain to grow and mature before it can cope with complex input or perform complex tasks. It also ignores the fact that talent and ability appear naturally in children, without the need for artificially intensive cultivation. There can also be a risk that parents may be serving their own unconscious agendas by trying to accelerate their child's development. In other words, it may be the parents' needs that are being met, rather than the child's. This creates the possibility of children being placed under unnecessary and potentially harmful pressure.

But that doesn't mean you should do nothing to nurture your child's potential, whether or not he seems to be gifted. Genuinely talented children still need encouragement and tuition if their promise is to be fulfilled, and all children are capable of responding in some degree to stimulation and good teaching. It is true, as the proponents of hot-housing say, that children's development can be accelerated in some areas. Development may be dependent on brain maturation, but the right kind of training and stimulation can certainly lead to faster and better learning. The important questions in regard to acceleration are how, and how much?

Children have a strong, in-built desire to learn. The best teaching follows the lead that the child gives by showing interest in a particular topic or activity. This kind of pupil-centred, individualised teaching maintains peak levels of excitement and motivation for learners of all ages. In addition, by allowing children to control the pace and scope of their own learning it shows respect for their uniqueness and dignity. A programme like this broadly answers the questions of how and how much in regard to accelerated learning, but because it demands so much in terms of time, expertise, and access to a huge range of resources and programmed materials, it does not yet exist. No parent or teacher, except under extraordinary circumstances, could afford to devote themselves solely to the development of a single child.

However, we have just entered a new era of information technology. Our grandchildren will have access to almost limitless knowledge through interactive, responsive, individualised computer-learning systems. Maybe then we will begin to discover the true boundaries of human potential.

In the meantime, for almost all children, be reassured that the normal range of preschool experiences will provide adequate opportunity for your child to reach his developmental potential.

Early intervention

Most children's development unfolds naturally and easily as they grow. As long as parents provide a reasonable amount of loving care and nurturing, their potential will gradually be realised, in the same way as a plant grows from seed, to shoot, to full-flowering maturity.

Not all children are so fortunate, however. Some are born with impairments of their sight or hearing, some with damage to the parts of the brain or spinal cord that control movement, and some with intellectual deficiencies that range from mild to profound. Some children are born with all their faculties intact, but into families where the effects of unemployment and poverty claim all of their parents' energy and coping resources, leaving little available for their children's needs. All of these children will require extra help if they are to develop to their full potential.

In Western countries, for the last 25 years or so, there has been a movement among child-health professionals to provide assistance for children with special needs as early in their lives as possible. This has been done in the hope that such intervention will minimise the long-term effects of conditions such as cerebral palsy, visual impairment, or intellectual disability.

Early-intervention efforts have been broadly directed towards:
- children born with an identifiable disability that has a physical cause, such as those mentioned above; and
- children born into home circumstances that place their future development at risk.

Early-intervention teams

Most Western countries today have health- or education-based agencies set up to assist children who have special educational or developmental needs. These agencies usually combine the expertise of a range of professionals, including paediatricians, psychologists, speech therapists, occupational therapists, and physiotherapists.

They recognise the importance of beginning work as soon as possible with infants and toddlers who will need extra help to reach their highest level of functioning. Each child is unique, and even with a recognised disability such as Down's syndrome or spina bifida, no one can accurately predict what each might achieve with the right support. The effects of some conditions are not curable, of course, but children with special needs deserve the maximum amount of therapeutic input throughout the years of growth in order to minimise the effects of their disability and maximise their potential.

Developmental checklists

The work of today's early-intervention specialists has been greatly helped by an explosion of research into and knowledge about infant and early childhood development over the last twenty years. This upsurge of interest in the field was given further impetus by a 1975 United States law that required appropriate education for all children with disabilities. This led educators to look much more closely at the fine details of normal human development so that they could accurately assess a child's current developmental status, then teach the next skill in the sequence of normal growth.

There are now reliable developmental checklists that detail the skills that children acquire as they grow from birth to school age, in the areas of motor development (or physical movement), language, intelligence, independence, and social skills. Armed with this knowledge, therapists and educators are in a strong position to help developmentally delayed children take the next step along the road to achieving their potential.

The cycle of disadvantage

Some children are hampered in reaching their potential not by physical, intellectual or sensory disability, but by social circumstances. In homes where unemployment and poverty drain the energy of parents, there may be little left over to dedicate to children and their development. Where there is little money or time for, or commitment to, all the activities and resources that stimulate the natural curiosity of toddlers and preschoolers, youngsters can arrive at school already well behind their peers from more affluent areas. School failure can then set the scene for discouragement, delinquency, and perhaps even eventual 'dropping out'. Often teenage parenthood then both completes, and begins again, the cycle of disadvantage.

There have been many attempts in the last 25 years to develop programmes to break this cycle of disadvantage, particularly in the United States. Probably the best known of these is the Head Start project, which began in the mid-1960s, continues today, and has been the model for many similar schemes. The experience gained from such projects, together with the results of research, has enabled early childhood workers to isolate the components that make the schemes successful.

In order to counteract the negative effects of social disadvantage, an early-intervention programme should be intensive, use skilled staff to train parents in understanding and stimulating their children's development, help parents deal with daily survival and family problems, and establish community support networks that will eventually be self-sufficient. Input from outside professionals is important, but helping parents to develop their own self-esteem, confidence and coping skills is crucial.

Common sense

It is well known that appropriate stimulation and learning experiences are important for children's development. Fortunately, children are naturally independent and self-motivated learners. In the early years, parents need to provide raw materials, opportunities, and guidance, but children will do the rest for themselves. As children grow older, parents need to be on the lookout for signs of special talents that can be nurtured more intensively, but in this parents need to be guided by common sense and a primary concern for their child's needs, not their own. For almost all children, the usual range of activities and opportunities that most parents provide is enough to keep them busy, stimulated, and, most importantly, happy.

If you feel that your child shows signs of outstanding ability, particularly in the area of overall intelligence, you can request appropriate assessment from school psychological services or from a child psychologist.

Parenting points

- Most parents recognise and understand that appropriate stimulation and learning experiences are important for children's early development.
- Many toddlers and preschoolers now take part in a wide range of interesting and enjoyable learning activities outside the home.
- Early stimulation is important and beneficial, but the physical maturation and growth of the brain sets a limit on how fast children can progress.
- Some children are born with outstanding natural talents in certain areas, but the signs of this soon become apparent to their caregivers.
- The belief that exceptional talent is made, not born, is the basis of accelerated-learning programmes or 'hot-housing'.
- Parents who embark on a hot-housing programme need to be clear in their own minds about whose needs the programme is actually meeting.
- The last 25 years have seen the development of successful early-intervention programmes for children with special developmental needs.
- For almost all children, the usual range of preschool activities is enough to keep them busy, stimulated, and happy.

3 Toilet training

Because it is such an important milestone, parents can become a little apprehensive about toilet training, having fears that if they don't get it right, their child might still be in nappies when she is 21!

But you can relax. Once small children become aware of what toilet training is all about, they actually want to be dry and clean. They want to be just the same as mum or dad, or their older brother or sister. All that's required of parents is to provide the right equipment and a bit of encouragement, and children will do the rest for themselves.

When to start

Toilet training is all about readiness. There are certain skills children need to have acquired if training is going to be successful, and it is well worth waiting until these skills are in place. Starting too early means unnecessary frustration for both you and your child.

In order to be toilet trained, a child first needs to develop an *awareness* of the sensations of urinating and passing a motion. She will demonstrate this by stopping what she is doing as she wees into her nappy, by showing obvious discomfort after she has filled it, or by displaying great interest in the stream and puddle if she wees without a nappy on.

A child also needs to have developed some *voluntary control* over the muscles that keep noxious substances in the right place until the right time. Unfortunately, there is no way of finding out for sure whether this has occurred until you actually start training, but about eighteen months is the earliest you can expect it.

The understanding and use of *language* is also an essential part of the toilet-training process. Before you begin, you need to explain to your child exactly what this new venture is all about, and there are some quite complex concepts involved in that. To cope with the whole procedure, your child needs to be able to understand and follow instructions, and be able to express herself at least in short phrases, such as 'Go potty now' or 'Do wees'. Most children won't have reached this level of language development until they are about two years old.

Taking all of these aspects of readiness into account, as well as the ability to take down knickers and trousers, most child-health professionals agree that two years is about the right age for most children to begin training. All children are different, of course, and some could be ready a little sooner, some a little later. If in doubt, it is best to wait.

Consider the season

Another point to consider is the weather. If your child decides that the time has come to perform, the fewer clothes that have to be removed to clear the way for action, the better. Training during winter means that there could be overalls to come down, then tights, followed closely by knickers. Things are much simpler during summer.

Ideally, toddlers shouldn't be wearing anything below the waist when training begins. This way, they can quickly see the association between the sensation of being ready to empty, and the end product. Once that link has been established, the next step is to reach the potty or toilet in time.

Asking your child to cope with undressing as well is a bit much, especially since, in the early days of training, there won't be much of a time lapse between early warning and release. And if your child has to run around with a bare behind, summer is the best time to do it.

As your child progresses, trainer pants can be used to absorb some of the results of the inevitable accidents, but be aware that your lounge suite and carpets are in for some punishment.

Provide models

When you decide it's time to start training, *show* your child exactly what's required. You can use a teddy or doll as the model, or provide a real live demonstration with yourself, your partner, or older siblings on the toilet. The desire to imitate, which is so strong in toddlers, can be a real help in the learning process. The example of a slightly older sibling or friend who has mastered the business can be particularly effective.

Give prompts, practice and praise

Start training with a potty. It is easier for a small child to mount, it is not as potentially frightening as the toilet, and is considerably more mobile when you go out and about. As your child graduates to the toilet, provide a step and a child-sized insert for the seat.

As with anything else you want to teach your child, you need to give lots of *prompts*, *practice* and *praise*. Once you have decided to begin, and have had a few 'undress' rehearsals, put her on the potty at regular intervals or ask from time to time if she wants to go. If the answer is 'yes', you're in business. If the response is 'no', remind her that if she wants to do wees or poos, she can do it on the potty.

It's usually easier to train for bowel motions than for urination, partly because there are fewer of them, and partly because you will probably have a good idea of when your toddler is likely to have a bowel motion. It can be helpful to sit her on the potty at the time things usually happen, which is often just after a meal.

Our parents' generation was encouraged to place even quite young babies on the potty after a meal. This was thought to 'train' them, but all it really did was take advantage of a natural reflex. The bowel begins to move of its own accord a short while after the ingestion of food, so while it is possible to catch a baby's motion if you time it right, this cannot really be called 'toilet training'.

Remember that punishment has no place in toilet training. There should only be praise for progress, or encouragement to try again next time. There's no need to use tangible rewards such as special treats, unless signs of progress are minimal.

There's also no need to rush. A well-known American book, written by Nathan Azrin and published in the 1970s, was called *Toilet Training in Less Than a Day* (Macmillan, 1975) — a title that probably said more about parents' needs than children's. It is certainly possible to toilet train children very quickly, but it is better to take things at the child's own pace. This is particularly the case with boys, who tend to train more slowly than girls. As a general rule, allow yourself a few months from start to finish, and be pleasantly surprised if you do it any sooner.

In the days of Freudian psychology, it used to be thought that successful toilet training was very important for later emotional adjustment, even as an adult. Not many psychologists today would see toilet training by itself as having such potential significance. Some anxious or perfectionist parents may put pressure on their toddlers to become clean and dry in the shortest possible time, but it is likely that such parents will be putting pressure on their children in other areas of their development as well. It is, therefore, the ongoing interaction between parent and child that is potentially harmful, rather than the single issue of toilet training.

Problems with older children

If your child is still having frequent daytime wetting 'accidents' by the age of about four, it would be sensible for her to have a medical check-up.

Soiling accidents past the age of toilet training seem to be more common among boys. Some boys go through a stage of passing motions into their pants when they are squatting at play, either indoors or outside. This may be a passing phase, which is once again best handled by prompting and encouragement, rather than punishment, or it may be an indication that the child is going to have ongoing problems with bowel control. A small percentage of boys do seem to have persistent difficulty in staying clean, even when a medical check shows no physical abnormality. This can take the form of a tendency towards constipation, where nothing happens for three or four days and then a large motion is passed, or the stools may actually become compacted and hardened in the bowel with overflow and leakage of semi-liquid material into the underpants.

In cases of chronic soiling past the preschool years, professional input is necessary. In my experience, a combination of appropriate medication, the right diet, and regular toileting that takes advantage of the bowel's natural rhythm, can be effective in most cases.

Loss of dryness and cleanliness after successful toilet training has been achieved can sometimes be due to psychological causes, but this is relatively rare. The arrival of a new baby in the house can sometimes cause it, as can some more serious events such as abuse. A sudden loss of bowel and/or bladder control that can't be explained on the basis of some obvious cause such as illness, and that lasts for more than about a week, needs professional assessment.

Parenting points

- Your child needs to be developmentally ready for toilet training. In particular, she needs to have an awareness of the sensations of urinating and passing a motion, some voluntary control over her bladder and bowel, and enough language development to understand and take part in the toilet-training procedure.
- The summer nearest your child's second birthday is a good time to start.
- Remember the three Ps: prompts, practice and praise.
- The fourth P — punishment — has no place in toilet training.
- Frequent wetting or soiling past the age of four needs medical assessment.

PART TWO
Problems at night

4 Night waking

A baby's cry cuts through sleep like a buzzsaw through balsa wood. And that's just what it's meant to do. Nature came up with a winner in designing an effective transmitter for babies to let parents know that a little attention would be nice — and right now if you wouldn't mind!

Nature also made sure that parents were equipped with a receiver tuned to just the right frequency for their baby's signals. Babies' cries have an in-built priority-one code for the adults who care for them, so other business is put aside until the message is attended to. It's just not possible for most parents to ignore their baby's cries. Parents feel uncomfortable until they have worked out what the baby wants, have met that need, and the crying has stopped. A baby's cry is what psychologists call an *aversive stimulus*: an unpleasant event that makes you feel good when it stops.

The trouble with babies is that they can't tell the time. They are quite likely to start transmitting distress signals even after their parents have knocked off work for the day, and are actually in bed asleep! And that's when the golden glow of parenthood can start to become a little tarnished. There are several different ways of dealing with night waking in babies discussed in this chapter, and parents need to choose the right approach for them and their baby.

When does it become a problem?

Most parents accept that their new babies are going to cry quite a lot, and a fair amount of that crying is going to take place at night. For one thing, the sleeping pattern of a newborn takes no account of whether the sun is up or down, and for another, whenever a newborn baby wakes up, he usually needs to be fed. So, parents should expect their sleep to be broken in the early months of a baby's life. But when can you hope to have a reasonable run of sleep, especially during the dreadful graveyard shift, those still and silent hours from midnight to dawn when nobody else in the neighbourhood seems to be awake except you and your baby?

Over the first few months, babies gradually adjust to life outside the womb, and to the rhythm of the sun. Their cycle of frequent short sleeps both night and day becomes a pattern of two or three longer daytime sleeps, more sleep at night, and longer periods of daytime wakefulness.

Average daytime sleeping time reduces from about seven-and-a-half hours to three hours over the first nine months, while average night-time sleep increases from nine hours to eleven hours. Bear in mind that these are average figures, so your baby could be sleeping more or less than this.

Unfortunately, those nine to eleven hours at night are unlikely to be in one stretch. Different studies of night waking have produced different results, but it seems that there is about a 75 per cent chance that your baby will be sleeping regularly and reliably right through the night by twelve months of age. On the basis of these figures, some night waking is reasonably common, and could be regarded as normal baby behaviour for much of the first year.

So when should you say 'Enough!' and call a halt to night-time room service? As with most of the big questions in life, there is, unfortunately, no definite answer. It depends partly on your patience, partly on when most babies are sleeping reliably through the night, and partly on how often it's happening. An occasional night-time squawk is a different matter from being woken every night, often more than once.

Taking everything into account, most of the professionals who deal with this problem would probably agree that after about six months there is unlikely to be any physical reason for your baby not to have settled into a pattern of sleeping through the night most of the time. To be absolutely on the safe side, if your baby is still disturbing your sleep at nine months and you don't like it, you are certainly justified in doing something about it.

Finding a solution

If you ask health professionals for advice, or read some of the many books available on the subject, you will get a range of suggestions about what you can do. Basically, however, there are three approaches you can take:
- Respond to the crying whenever it occurs
- Make a minimal response
- Don't respond at all

Responding at all times

The 'respond' school of thought is probably best represented by American paediatrician Dr William Sears in his book *Nighttime Parenting* (American Library, 1987). Dr Sears believes in a totally child-focused approach that includes prolonged breastfeeding and encourages parents to have babies and toddlers sleep with them. He believes that young children need to be 'parented to bed and parented awake'. In other words, a parent should be by their side until they fall asleep and whenever they awaken. Not surprisingly, Dr Sears also thinks that a young child's night-time cries should always be responded to, because of what he sees as the possible harmful psychological effects of not responding on both parent and child.

Dr Sears is probably right when he says that night waking in older babies would not be so much of an issue if they were in the parents' bed and were able to sense someone next to them as they stirred, then drift back to sleep reassured. However, many parents who have tried this method find that their own sleep is disturbed. Dr Sears suggests the sensible compromises of having either a cot with the side down placed right next to the parents' bed so that it forms part of one big sleeping surface, or a mattress placed on the floor by the parents' bed. He paints an invitingly warm and cosy picture of the attractions and benefits of family beds, but parents need to be aware that research on cot death has found that bed sharing is a risk factor to babies, especially if the mother is a smoker.

Not responding at all

A totally opposite approach to dealing with night waking, the 'don't respond' school, is described in *The Sleep Book* (Heinemann Reed, 1985) by Kathy MacDonald of the Leslie Centre, a family therapy clinic in Auckland, New Zealand. This system was developed as a way of helping parents who were left exhausted, angry and discouraged by their child's frequent and continual waking, or refusal to go to bed. It is based on the belief that after the age of about nine months, children are capable of sleeping through the night, and no longer have the kind of physical needs that parents must attend to promptly in younger babies.

The basic operating principle of this approach is that crying in the night is like any other behaviour; it is maintained and reinforced by achieving results. In this case, the desired result is having a parent around in the wee small hours! The 'don't respond' theory maintains that if, after the child reaches a certain age, parents refuse to go to him when he cries at night, the child will learn that crying doesn't work and will stop doing it. This approach differs from the previous one in that it considers the parents' needs to be as important as the child's, and argues that unless parents have the energy to be able to function effectively during the day, everybody in the family will suffer.

It takes the position that the day-to-day parenting of young children is hard work and demands a level of stamina and patience that is hard to find if you are physically exhausted. The relentless grind of long days and sleepless nights can take parents to breaking point, and drastic situations may require drastic solutions.

The 'don't respond' solution is drastic because it asks parents to fight against their instinctive urge to go to their child when he cries. It asks parents to listen to their child sob or scream, sometimes for hours, in the dark and stillness of the night, and not go in to comfort him.

There is plenty of evidence, however, that this method works. A study undertaken by Leslie Centre staff of more than two hundred families that used this programme showed a reduction in night waking over a four-week period from 95 per cent of the sample waking at least five nights a week to 78 per cent waking no more than twice a week. According to reports I have heard from parents who have tried it, these results seem a little pessimistic, and I think that most parents could expect to see a major improvement within three nights, with significant reductions in crying time each night.

Unlike Dr Sears, *The Sleep Book* encourages parents to teach their children to settle to sleep on their own. It suggests that, after comforting bedtime rituals, cuddles and kisses, the journey to the Land of Nod should be a solo one. Then if children do wake up in the night, they won't need their parents' presence to go back to sleep.

The 'don't respond' approach simply requires parents to not respond to their child's cries. That's it. Very simple, but very, very hard to do.

Minimal response or 'controlled crying'

In between the 'love 'em' and the 'leave 'em' philosophies is the minimal-response method of Australian paediatrician, Dr Christopher Green, described in his well-known book, *Toddler Taming*. Dr Green's 'controlled crying' technique involves the following steps:

1 Leave your night waker to cry for anything between three and ten minutes, depending on how tough you are.

2 Then go in to him, cuddle and comfort him until he quietens, put him back down, and depart.
3 When crying begins again (as it surely will), leave him to cry for *five minutes longer* than you did the last time.
4 Repeat steps 2 and 3, increasing the delay by *five minutes each time* until silence reigns.

If, after one hour of this, the child is still crying, Dr Green suggests considering sedation, although he doesn't make it clear who should take it — you or the baby!

Other writers have suggested variations, such as increasing the response delay and not cuddling the baby when you go to him. A similar, but more simple, technique is described in *My Child Won't Sleep* (Penguin, 1984) by Jo Douglas and Naomi Richman. They call their system 'checking'. It involves going to the child when he first starts to cry, reassuring him briefly, *without* cuddling or lifting, then tucking him in firmly and leaving, even if he hasn't settled. If the crying continues, they suggest parents wait for five minutes, then return and repeat the procedure. Keep doing this until the crying stops. This method requires fewer time-keeping skills than Dr Green's, but more endurance, because you need to hang in there until your child gives up and finally goes to sleep.

Choosing an approach

Judging by the number of books written about it, night waking is clearly a major problem for many parents. To put it quite simply, being deprived of sleep on a regular basis over a long period can be a form of torture, and the fact that the torturer is your own child doesn't make it any easier to bear. If you have ever felt like harming your baby because he won't stop crying and go to sleep, I can assure you that you are not alone. When exhausted parents joke that they felt like 'throwing the baby out of the window last night', it's very likely that there's more than a grain of truth in what they say.

Which method you choose to solve the problem will depend to a large extent on your feelings. If you think that letting children cry it out is cruel and inhuman, then no one will be able to convince you to try it. If you feel that your toddler's night-time cries always indicate a genuine need, then you will no doubt respond to them, and deal with your daytime tiredness as best you can. On the other hand, if there is no obvious reason for your nine-month-old to be waking more than once a night almost every night, you may be able to accept that it is no more than a habit — a learned behaviour — and treat it as such.

If you want your older baby to sleep through the night, then long-standing habits have to broken, and there is no easy way to do that. He will have to learn that crying without good reason after bedtime will not bring comforting attention from you. This means that you have to respond either minimally or not at all.

A huge amount of experimental evidence shows the quickest and most effective way to eliminate a learned behaviour is to withhold, completely and permanently, the rewards that sustain it. Learning theory says that the best way to stop night waking in children is not to respond to it at all, and that partial responding, such as 'controlled crying' or 'checking', is more likely to maintain the crying than eliminate it, because you are still rewarding your child by going to him when he cries. In fact, if you delay going to them, you teach them to cry more strongly, because the message you give is that if they really cry hard for five to ten minutes, then — 'Hey, about time, Dad! What kept you?'.

Some parents worry that ignoring their older baby's night-time cries could affect their baby's sense of trust, damage the bond between them, or even have some harmful effects on their child's self-esteem at a later age. This is extremely unlikely, for two reasons. First, it's important to keep things in perspective and realise that we are talking about only a few hours of distress in an entire childhood. Second, we need to be aware that babies are not mature enough to interpret events in this way or even to remember them for very long. They are far too young to interpret your not coming to them in the night as an act of rejection, and even if they did, lots of loving daytime attention from refreshed, patient and wide-awake parents should reassure them.

One method for helping children to sleep that I haven't mentioned in detail is medication. Nobody feels very comfortable about suggesting drugs as a solution for night waking in young children, but doctors may sometimes prescribe them if parents are under severe stress from lack of sleep and need relief for a few nights. Your doctor can advise you about the different medications available, their effectiveness and drawbacks.

Night waking in older children

With older children who won't go to bed or still wake up at night, the problem is not so much crying as getting out of bed. A favourite game for toddlers and preschoolers is to prolong the bedtime routine by asking for one more story or to stay up for a little while longer — or to come trotting back into the lounge after they have been tucked up and kissed goodnight.

The best way to deal with this is not to argue the toss, but, saying as little as possible, to return your child to bed. Try not to rant and rave or, even worse, laugh. Go into robot mode. Do this as often as it takes until your child gets the message that he will not be allowed to stay up after lights out. If your patience wears thin, your only other option is to tell your child that if he doesn't stay in bed, the door will be fastened in some way. Don't make this threat lightly, because once you have made it, you will need to carry it through. Having the door locked or fastened can be very distressing for some children, but remember that you are giving them a choice. If they stay in bed, the door won't be locked.

The same strategy applies for little ones who come to your bed in the middle of the night. If you don't mind them hopping in with you, that's fine. If you find that you can't sleep with a wriggling bundle of elbows and knees, then you need to be firm. As soon as you become aware of a little presence at your shoulder, tell him he has to sleep in his own bed and escort him back to his own room.

Do this as many times as necessary. If you have to, give him the choice of staying in his own bed or having the door locked. And if you find that you just don't have the willpower to fight these 2.00 a.m. battles, a reasonable compromise is to have a sleeping bag or duvet on the floor next to your bed that your child can use, rather than getting into bed with you. Your child then has the choice of being slightly uncomfortable sleeping on the floor next to you, or going back to the warmth and cosiness of his own bed.

Parenting points

- Over the age of nine months — at the outside — there is no physical reason why your baby should not be sleeping through the night on most nights.
- You have three choices in how you deal with night-waking in older babies and toddlers: respond at all times; respond minimally; or do not respond at all.
- Responding to crying is likely to maintain it.
- The minimal-response method has been promoted by a number of different writers, and has been shown to be effective.
- Not responding to your child's cries at all is very hard to do, and very distressing for everyone, but it does work. You have no reason to worry about your child's future emotional adjustment if you use this method.
- The final choice is over to you. If you are in doubt, talk to your family doctor.

5 Nightmares

Sleep is not the simple state that it seems to be. Every night we go through regular changes in bodily and mental activity without being aware of it. For our purposes we can say that there are basically two different kinds of sleep:
- active or 'rapid eye movement' (REM) sleep; and
- quiet or 'non-REM' sleep.

During REM sleep, our breathing and heart rates are faster and less regular than they are in non-REM sleep. Our blood pressure is higher and we have very little tone in our muscles. In fact, it is almost as if we are paralysed.

But the most distinctive feature of this kind of sleep is the rapid movement of our eyes, which is associated with dreams. If people are awoken during a REM period, they almost always report that they were having a dream. REM sleep is lighter than non-REM; that is, it is closer to waking awareness.

During non-REM sleep, our breathing and heart rates are slow and regular, our blood pressure is lower, and we make few body movements. In particular, there are no rapid eye movements. People woken during non-REM sleep do not report dreams in the sense of a dramatic story with characters and action, although some kind of vague thinking does seem to occur. It would be reasonably accurate to describe non-REM sleep as 'deep' sleep.

Sleep cycles

The different stages of sleep occur in cycles during the night. These cycles can be thought of as waves formed by the peaks and troughs of light and deep sleep.

Adults begin their sleep with a descent into a non-REM period. They then move up to lighter sleep, descend again into non-REM sleep, ascend to the first REM period of the night, and so on through to the morning.

In adults each cycle — from a REM peak through a non-REM trough to a REM peak — lasts about 90 minutes. This gives about four or five cycles during one night's sleep.

The amount of REM sleep increases with each cycle, so that our longest dreams occur just before we awaken. A REM period in the later part of sleep can be as long as 30 or 40 minutes. In contrast, the deepest non-REM periods occur at the beginning of sleep.

Adults spend about 20 per cent of the night in REM sleep and about 80 per cent in non-REM. The proportion, however, changes with age. For babies, the ratio is about 50/50, with the amount of REM sleep gradually reducing until, by late adolescence, it is about the same as an adult.

Sleeping babies also differ from sleeping adults in other ways. They begin their sleep with an REM, rather than a non-REM period, and the length of their sleep cycles is shorter, being about 40 to 50 minutes. Even babies in the womb seem to have sleep cycles from about the sixth or seventh month. But whether they actually dream (and what they might dream about!) is not known.

If you watch your baby carefully while she is sleeping, you should be able to notice the different sleep stages. During REM sleep, her breathing will be irregular, she may twitch and jerk slightly, and you will see her eyes move under the lids. In non-REM sleep, her body is completely still and her breathing is quiet and regular.

Night-time disturbances

Nightmares and night terrors

Young babies don't have nightmares, but they are reasonably common from toddlerhood up to the age of about six or seven. A nightmare is a dream like any other, except that it is frightening enough to wake your child, who then yells for help!

Nightmares, because they are dreams, occur during REM sleep. The content of children's nightmares, not surprisingly, has to do with things that frighten them during their waking lives: animals; monsters seen on television; being chased; the threat of injury or death. If a child has had a particularly distressing experience, such as being involved in an accident, or undergoing a painful medical treatment, this can cause recurring nightmares on the same theme.

Nightmares are relatively common, and some researchers estimate that as many as 20 to 30 per cent of children experience them at some time. They are usually the result of an upsetting experience and are not a sign that your child is psychologically disturbed. They need no treatment other than your reassuring presence.

Night terrors are not as common as nightmares, but they can be very frightening — for parents and child alike. Imagine this scene. You are awoken early in the night by a terrified scream from your child. You go into her room to find her sitting up in bed, sweating, eyes staring, heart racing and breathing fast. You try to comfort her, but she only mumbles incoherently, does not want your cuddles, and doesn't seem to be really awake. After several minutes, you manage to get her to lie down again and she is soon off to sleep. The next morning you ask her about what happened, but she has no memory of the event.

What this child experienced was not a nightmare, but a night terror. The major difference between a nightmare and a night terror is that a night terror is not a dream. In the most extreme cases, the child screams, sweats, and stares wide-eyed with a pounding heart at an unseen threat, but is still asleep. It is very hard to wake a child who is experiencing a night terror. If you manage to do so, she is usually unable to tell you what was frightening her, and is obviously confused about what has happened.

With nightmares, the child is usually already awake by the time you get to her, and has vivid recall of the details of the dream, which will also be clearly remembered in the morning. With night terrors, there is usually no recall at all.

The cause of night terrors is not really understood. They are somehow related to the switch from deeper to lighter stages of sleep, but how this can have such a dramatic effect on some children is a puzzle. Fortunately, only a small percentage of children experience night terrors, usually in the early to middle years of childhood. Some children may have only a few episodes a month, while a few may have them more frequently, sometimes even nightly. Not all night terrors are as dramatic as the example given above. They can range from restlessness and mumbling, to thrashing about and moaning, through to the 'full on' night terror described above.

There is no recognised treatment for night terrors, but treatment is usually not necessary because they occur only occasionally. There is some evidence that children who suffer from night terrors are more likely to experience them if they are stressed or fatigued. In some cases, night terrors occur regularly and frequently, sometimes even at about the same time each night. In this case, it has been found that waking the child about fifteen or twenty minutes before the night terror usually occurs will stop it from happening. The effectiveness of this method seems to be related to the disruption of the usual sleep cycle.

Dealing with nightmares

As with night terrors, nightmares usually only happen occasionally, and need no treatment other than on-the-spot cuddles and reassurance. Persistently recurring nightmares, however, do require some form of professional intervention. The major forms of intervention, which are probably best suited to children over seven years, are:

- Desensitisation
- Confrontation
- Therapeutic play and drawing
- Dream control

Desensitisation

Deep relaxation of the muscles has been found to be very useful in the treatment of daytime fears. In a method called 'systematic desensitisation', people are taught to relax deeply and then to imagine the things that frighten them, in gradual steps, from least to most scary. The same procedure has been shown to work with nightmares. For example, if the nightmare was about being attacked by an animal, it would be broken down into its various parts, like stills from a movie. The child would then imagine each part while maintaining deep relaxation, until she could picture the whole dream and remain calm.

For this method to be successful, the nightmares would all have to be on the same theme. The child would have to be able to recall some details of it, and would have to be old enough to understand and use the method — probably about eight years of age at least.

Confrontation

Young children can be taught to confront their nightmares in the daytime and so overcome their fear. If, for example, a child has scary dreams about a monster, teach her to say things like: 'Get out of here, you old monster! You don't scare me! You are just a dream. You can't hurt me!'. Give her practice in saying these things out loud, really believing them, and even in acting out fighting the monster and throwing it out of the house. When the child does this, she begins to feel she is in control of the nightmare and it loses its power to frighten her. Children as young as preschool age can be taught this method.

There are also some excellent illustrated stories available to help children confront their fears. They provide an enjoyable opportunity for you and your child to practise some bold behaviours and send those ghosts and ghoulies on their way.

Therapeutic play and drawing

Young children can also often deal with their fears through guided play. One three-year-old girl, who suffered from leukaemia, developed nightmares related to the often painful treatment procedures. She was helped by playing 'doctors', and used actual medical equipment on her dolls. In this way, she became less frightened of the equipment that was used in her treatment and her nightmares gradually disappeared. The same principle can be applied to other situations or imaginary creatures of which a child is frightened. Dealing with them in play can make them less scary.

Another method is to make a drawing of the frightening object and then tear it up. By drawing the object, say a monster, the child can begin to feel some control over it. By tearing it up, she symbolically destroys it. And while destroying it, she should say things like: 'That's the end of you, you rotten old monster! I can get rid of you, just like this!'.

Dream control

Some writers believe that it is possible to stop unpleasant dreams by thinking of them during the day frequently and saying: 'Stop! This is only a dream! Go away!'. You can teach your child to do this, especially at bedtime.

An alternative is to discuss with your child what happened in the nightmare, then get her to think of different ways in which the dream could have ended — that is, what she could have done in the dream so that it had a happy ending for her.

Chronic nightmares can be related to ongoing sources of stress in your child's life that may need to be addressed. The onset of nightmares can be associated with starting school; the arrival of a new sibling; failure at school; bullying; sexual abuse; or family arguments. If your child suffers from recurring nightmares, check for these possible sources of stress or worry in order to identify and eliminate them, if you can.

Remember the importance of such things as night-lights, cuddly toys and bedtime rituals like stories, songs, and prayers. But, in the end, the best cuddly toy in the world is probably you!

Sleepwalking

Interestingly, sleepwalking is part of a family of sleep disturbances that includes night terrors and sleeptalking. All these disorders have a number of features in common. They tend to occur early in the night during a non-REM period at a time of arousal from deep sleep to lighter stages of sleep. It is very hard to awaken children during an episode and they have no memory of it in the morning. The same child may suffer from more than one of the disorders and there is evidence that they may run in families.

One researcher has arranged these sleep disorders in order of intensity from sleeptalking, to sitting up in bed briefly, to sleepwalking, to thrashing about in bed, to a full-blown night terror.

Contrary to what most people think, none of these events has anything to do with dreaming. For example, a child who sleepwalks is not 'acting out' a dream. She is behaving automatically and without awareness, like a robot. She is using only very basic brain functions to get out of bed, walk around the house, and avoid obstacles.

Although the eyes of a sleepwalker are open, they are unseeing. Your child may give brief answers to questions, but she is not really thinking. It is as if her higher thought processes are switched off. A sleepwalker may be experiencing some vague, dream-like thoughts, but she is not expressing a vivid, story-like dream through her actions.

The best way to deal with a sleepwalking child is simply to guide her back to bed. There is nothing to be gained by waking her up, especially if she seems agitated. It is usually hard to wake a child from one of these episodes, and you may actually cause further distress if you keep trying to rouse her. Just encourage and guide her back to bed, where she will soon drift back to restful sleep.

If your child suffers from frequent sleepwalking episodes or night terrors, which are severe enough to affect the way she functions during the day, you may need to discuss the possibility of medication with your family doctor or a paediatrician.

Parenting points

- Nightmares are frightening dreams, and usually result from upsetting experiences.
- There are differences between nightmares and night terrors. Night terrors are not dreams, they occur in a different stage of sleep, they are much less common than nightmares, and they are part of a group of sleep disorders that includes sleepwalking.
- Occasional nightmares or night terrors need no treatment other than parental reassurance.
- If your child has recurring nightmares, search for a source of possible stress in her life, and seek professional help.
- If your child has recurring night terrors, once again search for a source of possible stress. Also, try waking her a short time before the night terrors usually occur.

6 Bedwetting

Sometime in their third year, most children achieve two major developmental milestones — they learn to use a potty, and to go through the night without wetting. By the age of three years, about 60 to 70 per cent of children are dry at night; by four, about 80 per cent; and by five, about 90 per cent. The biggest jump occurs between the ages of two and three, when nearly half of all two-year-olds achieve night-time dryness.

Remaining dry at night is often seen as part of toilet training, but it is in fact the result of the development and maturing of a child's nervous system, rather than something he learns to do. Children do need to be physically ready for toilet training, but there is much more of a learning component involved in achieving that skill. Night-time control occurs during sleep, so it is clearly not a skill that a child consciously acquires. Night-time dryness is not something over which a child has deliberate control.

The causes

Why some children take longer than others to gain control of their bladders at night is still not really understood. But while we do not yet know what actually causes repeated bedwetting (also known as 'nocturnal enuresis' or simply 'enuresis'), research has identified a number of factors that may be associated with it.

Sex differences

Boys are much more likely to be bedwetters than girls. The reason for this is not known, but girls are usually quicker to toilet train, and it may be that girls gain muscular control sooner than boys.

Family link

There is clear evidence of a hereditary factor involved in bedwetting. A child is much more likely to be enuretic if a close member of the family has a history of the disorder. Studies have shown that in about 40 per cent of cases, one of the parents was also enuretic as a child, and in about 70 per cent of cases a member of the extended family was enuretic.

Personality

There is some evidence that children who could be described as anxious, shy or introverted are more likely to wet the bed, but this is by no means usually the case.

Slow development

Bedwetting can be associated with slower than average overall development. For example, premature or low birthweight babies often develop more slowly than other children and have a greater chance of being enuretic.

Bladder function

The bladder function of an enuretic child can be different from that of other children. His bladder capacity may be measurably smaller than average, he may experience stronger and more frequent bladder contractions, and control over his sphincter (the bladder's stop-valve) may be relatively poor.

Some children who wet the bed may tend to urinate frequently during the day because of their small bladder capacity, and they may often need to go to the toilet urgently because of their strong bladder contractions and poor sphincter control.

Although there seems to be a relationship between bedwetting and bladder capacity in some children, those with normal bladder capacity may still wet at night, and even increasing a child's bladder capacity may not solve the wetting problem.

Depth of sleep

Many parents report that their bedwetting child sleeps very deeply and is hard to wake. It seems logical that a child who sleeps heavily is less likely to respond to signals from the bladder and is therefore more likely to wet. Research findings to date have not supported the hypothesis that enuretic children are harder to wake than others, but we should not entirely discount what seems to have been the common experience of many parents. For example, many parents report that when they have tried using a urine alarm, everyone in the family has woken up — except the child concerned!

Secondary enuresis

A small percentage of children begin to wet the bed after they have already achieved night-time dryness. This is called secondary enuresis, and may be associated with a traumatic event such as parent separation, moving house, being in an accident, or sexual abuse. Primary enuretics are children who have never had an extended period of night-time dryness.

The cures

There are several factors to consider in deciding when you should start to do something about your child's bedwetting. These include your child's age, whether he is reliably dry during the day, and your own patience.

First, effective treatment of bedwetting requires a level of involvement and commitment from a child that he is unlikely to have before the age of six, at the earliest. A child's co-operation is vital for a successful outcome, and it is very unlikely that a child younger than six will be worried about his bedwetting or be motivated to do anything about it. At that age, the problem is still very much yours, rather than his.

Second, a child must be reliably dry during the day before you can attempt to deal with night-time wetting. Night-time dryness requires the muscular control to hold on even when a child is asleep. If he is unable to remain consistently dry when awake, the chances of him doing so at night are fairly slim.

Third, your own patience and ability to cope with the continued inconvenience are important considerations. If you find your child's bedwetting frustrating and annoying (which it undoubtedly can be), you will probably want to sort it out as soon as possible. If you feel relatively relaxed about the situation, or if there is a history of bedwetting in the family, you may be prepared to put up with it for the time being, in the expectation that things will eventually improve.

It could be worth attempting to address your child's bedwetting problem earlier than six or seven if he has occasional dry nights. But if he is wet every night (and probably more than once a night in that case), try to relax about it and keep him in nappies until you are ready for the big campaign.

Methods that don't work

Research and experience have shown that some attempted remedies for bedwetting are ineffective. These include punishment, fluid restriction, waking or 'lifting', counselling and rewards.

Apart from the fact that punishment doesn't work, bedwetting is not a deliberate or conscious act, and a child should *never* be punished for it.

Restricting drinks before bedtime may make for a smaller wet patch, but is unlikely to solve the problem.

Waking your child to go to the toilet at your own bedtime (or 'lifting') probably won't stop the wetting, but even if it does, it is not helping your child to become independently dry.

Counselling is unlikely to have any beneficial effect on bedwetting, except in cases of secondary enuresis in older children.

The use of star-charts and other reward systems is often recommended, but these methods are not likely to work unless they are part of a total treatment package.

Methods that do work

But don't despair, there are methods that have been shown to be effective in treating bedwetting, including the urine alarm, bladder training, and medication.

Urine alarm

Studies have shown that the urine alarm is the most effective treatment for bedwetting. Between 60 and 90 per cent of children stop bedwetting after a first course of treatment. About 20 to 40 per cent of these may relapse within six months, but a majority will respond successfully to a second course. The alarm works by sounding a buzzer when urine comes into contact with a pad attached to the child's underwear or pyjamas. The purpose of the alarm is to wake the child as soon as he begins to wet, then to teach him to associate signals of bladder fullness with the sound of the buzzer, and finally, for signals from the bladder to wake him before the buzzer goes off. Urine alarms are available for rent or purchase from many pharmacies. Average treatment time is about two months.

Retention and control training

Some enuretic children have a smaller than average bladder capacity. It is possible to increase bladder capacity and strengthen the sphincter through retention and control training. This is done by getting children to drink more than they usually do, to hold on for longer before they go to the toilet, and to practise stopping and starting the flow when they urinate. These exercises are thought to stretch the bladder, thereby allowing it to hold more urine, to increase the strength of the sphincter, and to make the child more aware of signals from the bladder. This method has been shown to lessen night-time wetting in some children.

Medication

There are two drugs commonly used in the treatment of bedwetting. One is an anti-depressant, the other is an artificial hormone (desmopressin) designed to reduce the amount of urine produced by the kidneys.

At one time, anti-depressants were the most popular medication used in the treatment of enuresis. How they stopped bedwetting in some children is still not fully understood. Anti-depressants are now not so widely used, mainly because of their side effects, and because they can be extremely dangerous when taken in overdose.

Desmopressin (sold under the trade name of Minirin) is rapidly becoming the most commonly used drug for the treatment of enuresis. It has a reported initial success rate of about 60 to 70 per cent, has very few side effects, and seems to be quite safe. However, about 30 per cent of the children who respond successfully to the drug will relapse once they stop taking it. The advantage of desmopressin is that it begins to work almost immediately and so can be very useful for a special occasion or situation where night-time dryness is required, for example, at a school camp or during an overnight stay at a friend's place. Your doctor can advise you about the use of these and other drugs, including their risks and possible side effects.

A suggested programme

What follows is a suggested programme for the treatment of bedwetting. It includes a range of components that together can contribute to a successful outcome.

The main player in the programme is the urine alarm (or 'bed buzzer'). Most child-health professionals would recommend it as the initial treatment of choice for bedwetting. It has been used successfully for decades, is absolutely safe, has no side effects, and has the advantage that a child *learns* to be dry, rather than achieving dryness through drug therapy.

The other components in the treatment package are retention and control training, use of dryness targets, rewards, positive practice, motivation, and self-talk.

The programme requires levels of understanding, maturity and motivation that children are unlikely to be capable of under the age of about six or seven years.

STEP 1   *Make sure your child is motivated*

If your child is not motivated to be dry, the programme will not work. Discuss with him how he feels about his bedwetting, and if he would like to be dry at night. If the answer is 'yes', explain that it will take a while, but if he is prepared to stick at it, he *will* improve.

STEP 2   *Make sure you are motivated*

This programme demands a lot of energy, persistence and patience from parents as well. If, for any reason, you feel that you are not quite ready to take it on, wait until you are. Probably the number one reason for the failure of bedwetting programmes is that parents give up!

STEP 3   *Visit your family doctor*

It is only rarely that bedwetting is due to a physical cause such as an infection or a 'plumbing' fault, but you do need to check out all possibilities. Your family doctor may carry out a physical examination, take a sample of urine for analysis, and perhaps request an X-ray. It may then be suggested that you visit a specialist such as a paediatrician or a urologist (a doctor specialising in disorders of the urinary system). A medical check is particularly advisable in the case of children older than four years who are still wetting during the day as well.

STEP 4 *Discuss the programme with your child*

Your child needs to know how the programme works, why each component is included, and exactly what his role will be. As you discuss each step, listen to his suggestions and comments. It is important that he feels involved and committed, not pressured and compelled. Try to think of it as his programme, not yours.

STEP 5 *Keep records*

Maintaining a record of wet and dry nights will show you whether the programme is working. It can also help you to see if there is any pattern in the wetting — for example, is your child always wetting on the night before school starts, or after staying up late? As the weeks go by, the chart will become something that you can look back on and discuss, and signs of improvement can help you and your child maintain your motivation.

As part of the process of involving your child in his own treatment, ask him to draw up his own weekly charts, leaving enough space to put a star, stamp or sticker for a dry night. Leave wet nights as blank spaces rather than recording them as failures. In this way you are emphasising the positive not dwelling on the negative. Records will need to be more detailed once you start using the urine alarm.

STEP 6 *Targets and rewards*

Your child will need to work hard if he is to improve his bedwetting, and any genuine effort deserves to be rewarded. In discussion with your child, set a series of goals, extending from short-term to long-term. Aim first for one dry night, then two in a row, then three, five, ten, and, finally, fourteen. If your child has fourteen dry nights in a row he can be regarded as basically dry at night.

With your child, formulate a series of rewards to accompany this range of targets, beginning with something small and culminating in something really special. Make sure that the rewards are things he would really like, but are still within the limits of your budget — don't promise something you can't deliver. Record the rewards so that everybody remembers what was agreed upon.

For the earlier targets, up to ten days, make sure that he achieves each of them at least two or three times before moving on to the next one. When you get to the ten-day target, once will be enough.

And do I need to remind you about lots of praise and hugs for any signs of improvement? Of course not.

STEP 7 Rehearsals for night-time toilet runs

The action of getting out of bed and going to the toilet in the middle of the night needs to be almost automatic. Bedwetters usually don't get much practice at doing this, however, so they need to have a few practice runs before they go to sleep. Each night at bedtime, first get your child to pretend to be asleep, then to get out of bed and go to the toilet. Do this about five times each night, and turn it into a game by seeing how quickly he can do it.

STEP 8 Retention and control training

Retention training is intended to increase bladder size; strengthen sphincter control; and make your child more aware of signals from his bladder.

Begin by asking him to hold on for two minutes longer when he feels the urge to urinate. Increase this time by two minutes each day if he can manage it. He doesn't need to do this every time he wants to urinate, but should aim for at least two or three times each day. When he can hold on for 30 minutes after the initial urge, that's long enough. At the same time encourage him to drink more fluids — perhaps having two glasses where previously he would have had one.

To see if these measures are having any effect, you will need to measure his bladder capacity every two or three days. Do this by asking him to urinate into a measuring container after he has held on for as long as he can. Try to take the measure at the same time of the day, but remember there will be slight fluctuations in the amount from day to day anyway. Take the biggest measure of the week as the best indication of current maximum bladder capacity, and record it so you can watch for signs of improvement. A reasonable guide to average capacity is 30 ml for each year of age. For example, a target capacity for a six-year-old would be about 180 ml.

To further increase the strength and responsiveness of your child's sphincter, ask him to practise stopping and starting the flow *while* he is urinating. He should try to do this a few times whenever he goes to the toilet. Ask him to stop the flow, count to three, then start it again, but not at those times when he has been 'holding on'. It is difficult to do at first, but becomes easier with practice. This will eventually give him greater control over stopping the flow, even, we hope, when he is half asleep.

Begin retention and control training about two weeks before you start to use the urine alarm, and continue it while using the alarm.

STEP 9 *The urine alarm*

The final and most important component in the programme is the urine alarm. You can rent or buy one from a pharmacy.

The simplest type is one that has a moisture-sensitive pad, which is pinned to the underpants, and is battery operated. Whichever variety your pharmacy has available, read the instructions and follow them carefully.

It is particularly important that your child *wakes up* and goes to the toilet each time the alarm goes off. Wake him up yourself if the buzzer doesn't, but *he* is the one who has to switch off the alarm. This is necessary for effective learning to take place. Remember that it is going to take some weeks before he has learnt either to wake to signals from his bladder (that is, he has learnt to 'beat the buzzer') or to sleep through the night without wetting. Be prepared to lose some sleep yourself for a few weeks.

The usual criterion for pronouncing a 'cure' is fourteen consecutive dry nights. It improves the chance of a lasting cure, however, if you give your child a large bedtime drink after he has reached the fourteen-night standard. Keep doing this until he can achieve fourteen dry nights even with a bedtime drink. This procedure is called 'overlearning'. One writer has suggested building this bedtime drink into the programme from the time you start using the alarm. If you're brave enough to do this, it could be a good idea.

In his book *Waking Up Dry* (Writer's Digest Books, 1986), Martin Scharf describes a very good method for giving your child daytime practice in responding to the buzzer. Once a day, when your child wants to urinate, stand outside the toilet with the alarm. Ask him to practise stopping the flow in response to the buzzer, then trigger it manually once he has started. You might like to try this a few extra times on the first few days of using the alarm.

Keep a record not only of dry and wet nights, but also of the number of wets per night and the actual times at which the alarm goes off. This will help you and your child to see signs of improvement, such as fewer wets per night, and the time of wetting moving towards the morning.

Step 10 Self-talk

As part of the bedtime ritual, you should also encourage your child to use positive self-talk and imagery. Ask him to say, with great determination and firm belief, 'I *will* be dry tonight' or 'I *will* wake up to the alarm'. He should say these things at bedtime especially, but also when it occurs to him at any other time of the day. 'Positive imagery' involves imagining, as vividly and clearly as possible, every step in the process of going to the toilet at night — from feeling the first bladder sensations, to waking up, getting out of bed, and walking to the toilet. Your job is to coach and encourage your child in these things, and instil in him a real belief that they *will* happen.

What I have suggested here is a manageable programme that has a good chance of success. You will no doubt need to adapt some parts of it, depending on your child's maturity, your home circumstances, and what seems right for your family. But if there are no real signs of progress after one month of conscientious effort, give yourselves a break and try again in three or four months — a little bit of extra maturity may give your child a greater chance of success. Or, at this point, you may want to give medication a try. If so, speak to your family doctor.

Parenting points

- The cause of bedwetting is still not really understood, but there are a number of factors known to be associated with it.
- Bedwetting is more common in boys. It can also be associated with a family history of the problem, slower overall development, and personality type. However, it can occur without any of these associations.
- Some enuretic children are thought to have smaller bladder capacities than other children, to experience stronger and more frequent bladder contractions, and perhaps to have poorer sphincter control. However, having normal bladder capacity and function doesn't necessarily mean that a child won't wet.
- Parents often point to the depth of their child's sleep as an explanation for bedwetting. Research evidence does not fully support this hypothesis, but there is much anecdotal evidence in its favour.
- Treatment methods that *don't* work include punishment, rewards, fluid restriction, waking or 'lifting', and counselling.
- Treatment methods that *do* work include the urine alarm, bladder training, and medication.
- Children need to be at least six years of age to be able to understand and co-operate with a bedwetting treatment programme.
- Motivation, involvement and commitment are vital ingredients in a successful programme. Encourage your child to take responsibility for the programme, so that it becomes his. Your child must *want* to become dry at night before any course of treatment will be effective.

PART THREE
Behaviour Management

7 Toddler terrorism

Let's say that your two-year-old has just added some colourful crayon patterns to the lounge-room wallpaper, which don't really go with the rest of the decor. From your point of view this could seem like deliberately destructive behaviour, the first step on the road to her becoming a graffiti artist. From your child's point of view, however, the wallpaper simply provided an exciting opportunity to discover all the wonderful things a crayon could do on a big flat surface.

What is 'naughty' behaviour?

As parents we can save ourselves a lot of unnecessary stress and frustration if we understand and accept that much of the behaviour that we tend to call 'naughty' is just a result of children being themselves and doing what they are programmed to do. Young children are dedicated to exploring their environment, learning new skills, and becoming independent. They want to do things in their own way, in their own time. In other words, they have their own agendas and priorities, which, unfortunately, often don't match up with our own. And that's where the trouble usually starts.

Parental expectations

All parents realise that babies demand an awful lot of time and energy — most of it focused on the two ends of their alimentary canal — and that daytime and night-time activities must be juggled around their often erratic sleep cycles. Nobody would call a baby 'naughty' for crying or filling her nappy, because that's what we expect babies to do. In the same way, it is an essential part of a toddler's job description to get her sticky little fingers onto and into everything in sight.

So it is better to childproof the house before the onslaught begins, rather than trying to stop toddlers from doing what comes naturally. We should also resign ourselves to the fact that when preschoolers want attention, they need it *right now* (usually when we're on the phone), as they ask a constant stream of questions, boast about their achievements, and want us to join in their games. Expecting toddlers and preschoolers to wait is a bit like asking Niagara Falls to hold it for a minute.

Some parents expect young children to carry out chores reliably, and become cross when they do not. For example, expecting a preschooler to tidy up independently after play is unrealistic. Issues such as tidiness are adult ones, and are of very little importance to young children. If you want your young child to tidy up after herself, teach her how by doing it with her, not by growling if she does not do it.

Adapting your expectations

As parents, we can save ourselves much needless conflict if we accept that when little children annoy us, they are usually not being naughty, just busily going about their appointed role in their own delightful, unstoppable way. Of course children need to learn over time to control their feelings and impulses, and cope with frustration, but in the early years, we need to adapt *our* lifestyles and expectations to *their* needs, rather than the other way around.

There are several things parents can do to help them direct and respond to young children's natural curiosity and energy in positive ways.

Keep 'em busy

Busy children are happy children. They are also much less likely to get into mischief. If toddlers and preschoolers are not kept occupied, they will soon find ways of entertaining themselves, and we all know what that means. It's interesting that when the house suddenly falls silent, we usually tend to be suspicious rather than relieved!

Toddlers and preschoolers need a reasonably structured daily routine of activities selected from the following menu: indoor play, stories, meals and snacks, outdoor play, naps, television, a trip to the park, listening to music, shopping, visiting Nanna, and attending your choice of playgroup, daycare or preschool. Keeping little ones interested and occupied by providing a loosely structured plan for the day helps to make things go more smoothly, which is particularly important with that small number of very active boys who can push their parents' patience to the limit.

Children who have plenty of activities to keep them happily occupied are much less likely to become grizzly, demanding and defiant. Leaving children to amuse themselves for long periods, especially younger ones in the toddler to early-primary-school-age range, is a recipe for trouble. Bored children tend to be 'naughty' children.

Provide basic rules

Once your child is old enough to understand most of what you say to her, it is time for you and your partner to come up with some basic family rules. Probably the most important reason for having these is that they help parents to be consistent in dealing with problem situations. Consistency, and presenting a united front, are very important in dealing with children's misbehaviour, and even the most determined toddler cannot beat a resolute parenting team with a clear game plan.

Having definite rules also makes it easier for young children to monitor and control their own behaviour. First, young children actually prefer to have behavioural boundaries because it helps them to structure their world and gives them a sense of security. Second, our own behaviour is guided and controlled partly by self-talk — those things we say to ourselves when we are thinking about how to behave in a particular situation. It is helpful for young children to have a set of ready-made statements that they can 'play back' to themselves when they are deciding how to behave, such as 'We never write on walls', 'It's good to share your toys', or 'We don't swear in this family'.

Older preschoolers and early primary-school-age children go through a stage when rules such as this are seen as having great power, and they will say things such as 'We're not allowed to ...', 'Mum said we had to ...', or 'The teacher said we couldn't ...', as if they were immutable laws of the universe. Take advantage of this developmental stage by having your behaviour guidelines ready, and by using them frequently.

Give reasons

The evidence of research indicates that parents should explain the reasons for family rules to their children. If we discuss behaviour in terms of the positive or negative effects it can have on others or the environment, children are much more likely to develop their own personal code of conduct, which will guide their behaviour even when no one is watching.

But you need to be realistic about doing this. First, keep explanations simple, such as 'Don't pull pussy's tail. That hurts her.' Second, choose your moment. A lecture on ethics while your toddler is having a tantrum is a waste of time. It is better to discuss the issue briefly after things have calmed down. And remember, the shorter the child, the shorter the lecture!

Talk less, act more

There are many times in the daily life of a young family when things have to be done, right then and there. If a reasonable request and a brief explanation haven't produced visible results, it is time for you to stop talking, switch into robot mode, and make sure that things happen. There is always a place for discussion, argument and persuasion, but for families to operate effectively on a day-to-day basis, the bottom line has to be that parents rule, whether or not the children agree.

Children quickly learn to ignore parents who repeat their requests twenty times, or who threaten and shout, but hardly ever follow up with action. In my experience, many parents have been able to take back control from the small gangsters who have held them to ransom, simply by talking less and acting more.

Think before saying 'No' every time

'No!' is a word guaranteed to create friction between parents and children, and, unfortunately, it is the word that seems to come most easily to our lips. Saying 'yes' doesn't usually cause any problems (unless a parent has just caved in to whingeing or other pressure tactics), but try to pause a little before automatically giving the thumbs down.

Children are dependent on their parents, and the younger they are the more dependent they will be. Being dependent means asking for things, and constant demands from children can be very wearing. The simplest response to the torrent of requests can become 'No' or 'Not now' or 'I'm busy'. Sometimes that's fair and necessary, but if 'No' becomes your usual, automatic response, you must expect storms of protest.

A hasty, unthinking 'No!' can sometimes leave you in the awkward situation of having to defend an indefensible position, because you have turned down what was actually a reasonable request. You then have the unenviable choice of having to go back on your word, or of hanging in there and earning the undeserved label of 'meanie'. So, before you buy into a fight, ask yourself if it's really necessary to put the gloves on.

Think before you ask

If your child is inclined to be defiant, save your energy for the important battles. Don't ask her to do something unless it's important. For the time being, try to forget about minor issues such as tidiness and manners.

Think before you ask, and if the request is important don't back down. Make sure that your child complies. But try not to go into combat unless the issue is important and you intend to win.

Ignore provocation when you can

Ignore as much provocation from your child as you can. Paying attention to tantrums and whingeing only maintains and reinforces them. And ignoring means exactly that. Don't make eye contact.

Say nothing. Go about your business as if your child wasn't present. Walk out of the room if necessary. And if you are followed, go to your bedroom and shut the door.

Keep this up until your child begins to behave appropriately and *only then* switch your attention back on. The message must be clear: 'You will not get what you want through tantrums. I do not negotiate with terrorists. Behave nicely and then — just maybe — we can talk'.

There are two behaviours you can't ignore: hurting people and damaging property. If your child acts aggressively or destructively, you must intervene quickly and decisively, preferably with time-out. Because time-out is such a useful and important behaviour-management technique, it is discussed in detail in the next chapter. It is the treatment of choice for serious misbehaviour in children aged from about three years.

Be prepared for tantrums

Your first response to tantrums should be to ignore them, as described above. The louder and more outrageous the tantrum, the further away you should go. Don't surrender. Start to pay attention only when the behaviour once again becomes appropriate.

The only exception to this rule is if the behaviour becomes destructive of property or hurtful to others. Then the time-out rule applies.

Tantrums in public are naturally more difficult to deal with. If you feel brave enough, walk away. If this leads to personal attack or out-of-control behaviour, either abandon the outing and go home in icy silence, or use the car as a makeshift time-out area (with you in attendance of course).

Some writers have suggested hugs as a remedy for major tantrums. This works sometimes, but it can be physically difficult to do and you run the risk of rewarding unacceptable behaviour with cuddles.

Use distraction

Remember that the younger the child, the more likely it is that distraction will defuse a potential conflict situation. For two to three-year-olds, judicious distraction, cunningly and artfully employed, can be a parent's best friend!

Notice good behaviour

Always be on the lookout for good behaviour that you can acknowledge with specific praise ('Thanks for picking up your toys. That was a big help.'), a smile, or a hug.

Have a positive attitude

Toddlers can spot an indecisive parent at one hundred paces. Be confident. Be strong. Believe you will win — and you just might.

Parenting points

- Understand that young children are programmed to explore their environment, develop new skills, and assert their independence. Most often they aren't being naughty, just doing what comes naturally.
- Be realistic. Adjust your expectations and lifestyle to your child's developmental level.
- Keep small children busy. Busy children are happy children. You can't expect them to entertain themselves for very long without getting into mischief.
- Children need rules and limits. Provide the security of clear behavioural boundaries, and be as consistent as you can in enforcing them.
- Think before you ask your child to do something. If she is inclined to be defiant, don't ask her to do something unless it's important. When you do ask, make sure it happens.

- Talk less, act more. Don't repeat your request twenty times before you take action. Ask once, warn, then act. Giving reasons and explanations is a good idea, but keep them brief.
- Don't give in to toddler terrorism. Ignore whingeing and tantrums. Say nothing, look the other way, walk away. Respond only to reasonable behaviour. Don't ignore destruction or aggression.
- Use time-out for serious misbehaviour (see Chapter 8).
- Distraction is the best behaviour-management technique for toddlers.
- Always try to notice good behaviour and acknowledge it.

8 Time-out

Because most children are strong-willed and independent, there will often be times when they won't do what you want. There will be a clash of wills. Push will meet shove. But, in the end, the big guys have to stay in charge.

There is one very useful technique, which has been around for many years, known to most of us as 'time-out'. An earlier version, recorded in old storybooks, was when children had to sit in the corner if they were naughty. And probably for as long as the human race has lived in houses, parents have been bellowing to their offspring: 'Go to your room!'.

Over the last 25 years or so there has been a lot of research done into behaviour-management methods, and time-out is one that has been shown to be effective, particularly in dealing with defiance and aggression.

What makes time-out so effective? First, time-out puts a sudden stop to negative or hostile parent–child interactions and gives everyone a chance to calm down before things get out of hand. Second, time-out isolates a child and removes him from a major source of enjoyment and reward — family life. It delivers a simple but powerful message: 'Your behaviour is unacceptable, and we will not let you take part in our normal family activities until you change it'.

Removing a child from family activities for a period of time is a serious step to take, so time-out should be kept for reasonably serious misbehaviour, such as defiance, destruction and aggression.

Use time-out only for those behaviours that you cannot accept or overlook in your child.

Removing parental attention

With very young children, up to the age of about three years, most so-called 'naughty' behaviour can be managed by distraction, ignoring, or a firm verbal reprimand. Ignoring can be a useful method for responding to mildly disruptive, annoying behaviour like whingeing, cheekiness and tantrums, but it is often not used as effectively as it could be.

Remember, ignoring means paying absolutely no attention to your child in any way until the misbehaviour stops. It means that you must act as if he is not there while he misbehaves. Don't look at or talk to him while the misbehaviour continues, but be ready to respond as soon as his behaviour becomes acceptable again.

Parental attention is a powerful reward for children, and completely removing it is unpleasant for them. Total ignoring is really a form of time-out, except that instead of removing your child from the scene, you remove yourself, without actually leaving the room. If your child is extremely persistent in trying to regain your attention, you can physically remove yourself by going to your own room and shutting the door. In other words, you 'time yourself out' from them.

Time-out procedure

But back to the basic time-out procedure. First, make sure you give a clear, concise instruction to your child about his misbehaviour. Get his attention and make eye-contact. Use a firm, but not angry, voice. For example, 'Matthew, I want you to stop annoying your sister. You can see that she's getting upset'.

If he stops at this point, praise him for complying and carry on with your business. If he doesn't stop, warn him: 'Matthew, if you don't stop, you'll have to go to time-out'. If he still doesn't stop at this point, tell him to go the time-out area you have previously agreed on. If he goes to time-out on his own, that's fine. If he doesn't, walk towards him without saying anything. If that gets him moving, fine. If it doesn't, put your hand on his shoulder or arm, guide him firmly to the time-out area, and shut the door behind him. If he protests, remind him that timing doesn't start until he's quiet. Once the time is up, open the door and tell him that he can come out. Some children refuse to come out at this point, but that's okay — it's their choice. If shutting the door seriously upsets your child, it can be left ajar. If your child refuses to stay in time-out, however, you may have to give him the choice of either staying put or having the door locked. This is preferable to playing tug-of-war on the door handle, which just teaches your child to resist you physically.

Location of time-out

Where is the best place for time-out? Some people advise that it should be a boring, unstimulating place such as the laundry or bathroom, but these rooms can create problems of their own. My feeling is that the location of time-out is not as important as the fact that your child is being isolated from family life and your company until he is prepared to behave acceptably. So, even though there may be plenty to occupy and interest him in his own bedroom, it doesn't really matter if you use it for time-out. With preschoolers, a designated area like a chair or mat can also work well.

Duration of time-out

How long should children spend in time-out? The general principle is that it should be as brief as possible. As with any punishment, the longer it lasts the less effective it is likely to be because children will see it as unfair and become hostile. Most writers suggest about three to five minutes as the ideal, with timing to start when the child is quiet. A good rule of thumb is one minute for each year of age.

Something else to consider, however, is how long it will take *you* to calm down. If you are still angry about the incident, it's probably better to leave your child in time-out until you are able to interact with him in a reasonably calm and pleasant way.

With school-age children, it may be appropriate to offer them the choice of coming out when they are ready to apologise and/or behave appropriately. This option is useful because it asks children to reflect on their own behaviour and make a decision about accepting responsibility for changing it.

Parenting points

- Time-out can be an effective way of responding firmly to children's misbehaviour without the use of physical punishment.
- Time-out can be used with children over the age of about three years.
- Before you use time-out, be clear about how the procedure works. Explain it and discuss it with your child beforehand so he understands what the rules are.
- Use it only for serious misbehaviour, because the more you use it, the less effective it will be.
- Don't worry too much about the location of time-out, and make it as brief as possible.

9 Smacking

Parenting issues don't usually attract the attention of the news media, but there is one topic that is guaranteed to be the subject of much public discussion over the next few years: whether physical punishment of children by their parents should be made illegal.

Thirty years ago, this proposal would have been almost unthinkable. In recent times, however, there has been a steadily growing movement in many Western countries against the use of corporal punishment against children. There is already the precedent that prohibits corporal punishment in schools. Is it just a logical extension of this to legislate to prevent parents from hitting their children? Or is smacking our children at home in some way different from teachers caning them at school?

By any other name...

Is 'smacking' different from other forms of hitting? In most societies it is illegal for adults to hit other adults to control their behaviour. It is now accepted that the use of physical force is not an acceptable way for adults to sort out their disagreements. So why do many parents still condone the use of physical force with children?

It may be that the true character of physical punishment is disguised or softened by the language we use. For example, when many parents talk about 'disciplining' their children, what they often mean is 'smacking'. Even the word 'smacking' minimises the nature of the act of 'hitting' children to punish them.

When you take an objective, realistic view of smacking, it is surprising how many of us condone it as an acceptable parenting practice. We do everything we can for our children, go out of our way to protect them from pain, suffering and illness, and yet in many cases knowingly and deliberately inflict pain on them when their behaviour annoys or challenges us. If we love and respect our children, shouldn't we try to use every other possible form of discipline rather than physical punishment? Why is it not okay to hit any adult in our society, but okay to hit our own children? Is it a parent's right to smack, as some believe?

Does smacking work?

Perhaps the reason some parents smack children is because it seems to be an effective way to change their behaviour. It is our responsibility to teach children appropriate and acceptable ways to behave, and to protect them from danger, such as running onto roads. When all else fails, some might say, we must be able to use physical punishment as a final deterrent. But does it work?

In my experience, the answer is 'No'. The parents who come to see me about problems with their young children's behaviour invariably say that they have 'tried everything', including physical punishment. They tell me that smacking doesn't work and that the results are never what they were after: 'It just makes her worse', or 'She says it doesn't hurt', or 'She just tries to hit me back'. So the evidence for the effectiveness of smacking as a method of changing children's behaviour is not good. I have concluded that for most children, smacking is unnecessary as a means of controlling behaviour. And for the small percentage of very difficult children, where smacking sometimes seems to be the last remaining option, it doesn't work.

There is no doubt that hitting creates feelings of fear, anger and resentment within children — feelings that undermine what we are trying to achieve. Imagine how you would feel if you made a mistake at work and your employer not only shouted at you but hit you. Would you be inclined to listen carefully and change your behaviour accordingly, or would you become angry, shout back, and suggest where he might file his criticisms?

Children respond in the same way. The negative feelings created by physical punishment get in the way of a child's ability to learn new ways of behaving. At best, all you can hope to achieve is superficial obedience, with no real understanding of or commitment to the attitudes and behaviour you are trying to instil. If we want our children to behave according to our values and standards in a way that will make us proud of them, and not just to avoid punishment, we need to have patience and perseverance. Smacking is the easy way out, and like any quick and easy solution, it is unlikely to provide the result we really want.

A smack-free zone

If you feel uncomfortable about smacking your child and would like to avoid it, the first questions that probably come to mind are: 'What else can I do?' and 'How can I make my home a smack-free zone?'

Avoid unnecessary conflict

The first step is to avoid unnecessary conflict and reduce the number of situations in which a power struggle might surface between you and your child. There are a number of ways to do this (see Chapter 7), including keeping your child busy; being reasonable and realistic in your expectations; and thinking before you say 'No'.

Be clear, firm and consistent

Smacking is usually the end result of a child failing to carry out a parent's request, or breaking an important family rule. To increase the chances of your child complying with your requests:

- Don't ask your child to do something unless you really want it done, and are prepared to follow through to make sure that it is. If you ask, mean it.
- Be fair in your requests. Children aren't our slaves.
- Get your child's attention before you ask her to do something. Throwing a request over your shoulder to a child hypnotised by the television is a waste of time.
- Make your requests brief and clear.
- Ask once, warn, then act. If you are prepared to repeat yourself six times before you start to become frustrated and take action, don't complain that your child will never listen to you.
- Rules should be simple and kept to a minimum. If your children are old enough, involve them in a discussion about what the rules should be. They are more likely to comply with rules they have played a part in making.
- Be as consistent as humanly possible in enforcing rules and requests.

Plan ahead

Good ways to avoid excessive punishment of any kind include having a range of consequences available beforehand, and waiting before you decide what the punishment will be. How many times have you fallen into the trap of reacting angrily to misbehaviour, punishing excessively in the heat of the moment ('That's it! No television for two years!'), then regretting it when you've calmed down?

A better strategy is to spend a little time with your child — if she's old enough — deciding on a series of consequences for unacceptable behaviour. These could include doing without television or pocket money for limited periods, extra chores, time-out and being grounded (for older children), depending on the seriousness of the offence. Once you've decided, write them down. Then, when and if the occasion arises, instead of going 'over the top' in a rage, you can refer to the list and choose a suitable penalty. As an extra safeguard, tell your child how you feel about her misbehaviour, and that you will let her know in a while what the consequence will be. This gives you a chance to simmer down and choose a punishment to fit the crime, as well as making it much less likely that you will react in a rage and lash out physically.

Managing your anger

Despite all precautions, there are times when children are deliberately defiant, cheeky or destructive. When this happens, how can we control that first surge of anger, or perhaps the impulse to hit?

First, make a decision about whether hitting your child is acceptable to you as a form of punishment. If the answer is 'no', you will need to be mentally prepared for situations that are likely to make you angry enough to hit. Think about the things your child has done that have led you to smack in the past. Go over those situations in your mind and rehearse a new response, which will include the following four steps:

1 Identify the situation as creating a smacking risk by saying to yourself: 'I have to be careful here — I might hit'. Be particularly aware of the times you are under stress.

2 Express your feelings in words, not actions. Use an 'I' statement to let your child know how strongly you feel about what they've done. 'I am very angry (hurt, disappointed) about what you did. You know what the rules are about that'.

3 Remove either your child (or yourself) from the situation so that you can cool down: 'I want you to go your room until I decide what I'm going to do about this'.

4 Take as much time as you need to allow you to come back and deal with the situation without excessive anger.

Non-smacking as a goal

As parents we have to be realistic and accept that there will be times when our patience is pushed beyond the limit and we will be likely to smack our children. I readily admit that I smacked my own children in anger when they were younger, but I wish I hadn't, mainly because I now realise how unnecessary it was. Non-smacking should be a goal that we work towards in our parenting, even though, because we are human, we may never be able to achieve it completely.

Parenting points

Although I would urge parents to avoid smacking children as part of their discipline programme if possible, the decision is ultimately a conscience one for individual parents. It may be useful, when examining this issue within your own family, to ask yourself the following questions:
- Is smacking different from other types of hitting?
- Do parents have the right to smack their children?
- Is smacking necessary?
- Does smacking work?
- Could you manage your child's behaviour without smacking?

PART FOUR
Conflict

10 Aggression and anger

Acts of aggression and violence feature in the media every day. Much attention is now focused on violence within the family, and anger-management groups, particularly for men, have become widely available.

Many children are referred to child and family centres for behaving aggressively and having difficulty in controlling anger. What causes aggressive behaviour in children, and what can parents do to reduce the chances of anger and aggression becoming problems for their children?

Causes of aggression

Children seem to be equipped with a range of behaviours that they use to protect their territory and property. For example, a 2-year-old child may direct a barrage of hurtful behaviour towards a newly arrived sibling. This may include pinching, pushing and biting, and may be carried out both openly and secretly, for no other reason than to give the newcomer the clear message: 'Go away — I don't want you here'.

Playgroups and preschools can also be the scenes of toe-to-toe combat when the desire for a toy is stronger than the patience to wait for it, or when verbal negotiation hasn't worked. Toddlers and preschoolers can lash out at their parents' kneecaps when things aren't going their way, and even babies seem to enjoy yanking a handful of hair, or squeezing a fistful of nose.

Aggressive behaviour in little children is usually either an expression of frustration, a way of saying 'Keep off — that's mine!', or a way of getting what they want when words fail them. The specific behaviours of hitting, pinching, or biting seem to come naturally, with little or no coaching.

Aggression can sometimes get you what you want, and a child who has achieved success with a shove or a thump learns to use these methods whenever his wishes are frustrated. Aggression can then become his preferred strategy for solving all sorts of problems.

Children with delayed language development or speech difficulties may also use 'direct action' methods to achieve their aims because their verbal communication skills are inadequate. In such cases, frustration at not being understood can add potency to the mixture, making it even more explosive.

Some children, though, just seem to be born with more than their share of anger. They are irritable as babies, very demanding as toddlers and preschoolers, and seem to have a very short fuse — the slightest thing will set off a tantrum or a whirlwind of shouting, throwing and slamming. Some children's temperaments are naturally on the fiery side. This can be part of the Attention Deficit Disorder (ADD) or 'hyperactivity' syndrome, which includes a high level of physical activity, a short attention span, and a low tolerance for frustration (see Chapter 13).

What can you do?

An aggressive child needs specific guidance and support, which you can provide in a number of ways.
- First, have a clear rule that aggressive, violent behaviour is not acceptable in your family.
- Second, avoid exposing your child to examples of aggressive behaviour, including your own. If your temper is explosive, you

may be providing your child with a real-life model of how to use anger to get results. Television violence can encourage a child to learn aggressive behaviours, but the effect is not simple and direct. A reasonably placid and peaceful child will not automatically be turned into an aggressor by watching cartoons containing violence. However, research does show that naturally aggressive children seem to be more interested in violent programmes and may be more inclined to copy them. If your child is inclined to be aggressive, censor his television viewing.

- Third, make sure that aggressive behaviour is never rewarded. Return the toy that was captured in a snatch-and-grab raid. Give lots of love and sympathy to the victim of a hit-and-run attack, and a cold shoulder to the aggressor. The only rewards for aggression should be time-out and an apology to the victim. Ignore tantrums, but not aggression. There should always be a negative consequence for aggressive behaviour.
- Fourth, stress the need for words rather than action, saying rather than doing. Good communication skills reduce the need for aggression. Teach your child to ask and negotiate, and remind him about them when conflict looms.
- Finally, reward co-operative behaviour with praise, hugs, and stamps or stickers. Be on the lookout for sharing rather than grabbing, asking rather than snatching, and words rather than hitting. Reinforce these positive behaviours by noticing them and commenting on them.

Anger management

Children older than about seven years who have a definite, ongoing problem with aggression and anger are old enough to start learning anger-management techniques. The following suggestions may help you teach your child to manage his anger in more positive ways:
- Help him to *recognise the warning signs that anger is coming*. These include bodily signals such as a raised voice, clenched fists, a feeling of tension in the muscles, and angry thoughts.

- Prepare him to be alert to *situations that may lead to angry outbursts*, such as being teased by other children, making mistakes in class, and losing in a game. Once children are aware of the situations that tend to make them angry, they can be prepared for them and deal with them more effectively.
- Teach him *strategies that will help to divert his anger*, such as leaving the scene of a confrontation, or seeking out an alternative activity (preferably something energetic).
- Help him to practise using *self-talk to control his anger*. This is probably the most useful technique for controlling angry outbursts. Effective anger management ultimately depends on self-control, and self-control is based on self-talk — what we say to ourselves in our heads. An angry child is like a sky rocket with a very short fuse, and once the fuse has been lit, it can only be extinguished by what he says to himself. For example, 'Uh-oh! I think I can feel anger sneaking up on me. I'd better be careful here. If I lose my cool again, I'll be in big trouble. It just isn't worth it. I've got to calm down and find some other way of working this out'.
- Teach him to negotiate and *use words rather than actions*. Ask him to think about situations that often lead to conflict, then get him to role-play (or act out) behaviours that will defuse the situation. This is the essence of effective anger management and requires the use of words rather than direct action. But it can be difficult for children who have learnt to shoot first and ask questions later. So it is very important to help your child to practise responses in situations that tend to make him lose his cool.
- In a special book get your child to *record 'victories' against anger* — that is, to write about the times when he has kept the impulse to explode in check. This will help your child realise that he is beginning to gain control of his anger, rather than the other way around. It will also help him to be more aware of the strategies he has used to defeat anger, the message being that if he's done it before, he can do it again.

Mr Mad

With children from about the age of seven years who have a chronic problem with anger management, I often tell a story that uses the components listed above, but in a way that captures the imagination of the child and his family and gives him new energy to win the battle against anger. The story I use is based on a nasty, imaginary creature called Mr Mad, who sneaks up on unsuspecting children, takes control of them, and makes them do terrible things, such as yell at their parents, have tantrums, throw things, swear, and slam doors. This story can be modified to match each child's situation and can use the kinds of events that have actually occurred in relation to his anger. I often draw a picture of Mr Mad, or ask the child to do so, to help objectify the 'enemy'. This story can be a creative and fun way to help a child develop strategies for controlling the angry forces (Mr Mad) inside of him. It can help him to:

- recognise the *signs* that Mr Mad might be lurking about;
- be alert to *situations* where Mr Mad might try to take control of him;
- be aware of *strategies* that he has used in the past that have helped him to defeat Mr Mad;
- *say* things to himself to help bolster his courage and determination not to be beaten ('I'm not going to let dumb old Mr Mad boss *me* around anymore!'); and
- record any *victories* against Mr Mad.

This approach can energise and encourage children and parents who are becoming demoralised and depressed by the negative effects of chronic anger. There is no reason why you should not try to use this method yourself, but it is likely to have more impact and be more effective when implemented by a professional counsellor or therapist.

Parenting points

- Aggressive behaviour seems to come naturally, even to very young children, as they attempt to protect their territory or acquire booty.
- Aggression can become a learned response to frustration if it is effective in achieving a desired outcome.
- To prevent this happening in younger children, have a clear rule against aggression your family, don't model it yourself, make sure it is never rewarded, teach good communication skills, and notice co-operative behaviour.
- Children older than about seven years who have a chronic anger problem can be taught anger-management skills.

11 Sibling rivalry

Many parents worry about how their first-born child will react to having a new baby in the house. The newcomer is bound to absorb lots of the energy, time and loving attention that Number One Child has monopolised for as long as she can remember. It is no wonder ,then, that there is a very good chance that she will be less than happy about the arrival of a competitor.

A toddler's-eye view

When parents think about having a second child they often imagine her not just as a sister for their first child, but also as a resident playmate and friend. Many parents have golden visions of the two of them running or biking through the park, or walking off to school together.

Unfortunately, a young child's perspective is likely to be somewhat different. This new baby she has heard so much about is probably going to be a big disappointment. First, it's going to spend a lot of time just sleeping. Second, if it's not sleeping it'll be crying. Third, if it's crying Mum and Dad will probably drop everything else to attend to it. Where's the fun in that?

Your love, attention and comforting presence are vital to your toddler. Her world revolves around you, not just because you care for her physical needs, but because you form the foundation of her sense of security in the world. Having to share you with someone else is unlikely to delight her.

You may already have experienced this with your first-born child when you and your partner have been cuddling or kissing — only to find an angry toddler trying to push you apart! To your toddler, a new baby can be like a rival and challenger, a threat to her warm and secure world, a dark cloud passing over the sunshine of your attention. And what is any red-blooded toddler going to do when her territory is under attack? Fight back, of course.

Your first child's anger may be directed towards you, because you are responsible for the arrival of this interloper. There may be more tantrums, tears and sulks than usual, and perhaps even direct physical aggression towards you. Sometimes the new baby will be the target of her attacks, which could take the form of hitting, pushing, pinching, poking, scratching or biting. These may occur when you are attending to the baby's needs, such as when you are breastfeeding, or simply at random whenever the opportunity presents itself.

Some children may not display this kind of behaviour at all until the new arrival becomes mobile and begins interfering with their toys or activities.

All children have different temperaments, however, and some toddlers react not with anger, but by becoming clingy, demanding, quiet or withdrawn. Some can revert to earlier developmental behaviours such baby talk, or wetting and soiling, even though they have been toilet trained for some time.

Before the big event

Most parents are well aware of the possibility of an emotional fallout and a behavioural backlash on the arrival of the new baby and do their best to prepare their first child for the event. Fortunately, Mum's changing shape gives plenty of opportunities for talking about what it will mean to have a new baby sister or brother. Dusting off the pram and repainting the cot can provide your toddler with visible evidence of some of the changes that will occur. There are also many books written for children on the subject, which you can read and talk about both before and after the baby's arrival. Looking after a friend's or relative's baby for a morning or afternoon can help to give toddlers some first-hand experience of what it will be like when the new family member takes up residence.

After the baby arrives

Unfortunately, because toddlers and preschoolers tend to live very much in the present, the positive effects of talking about an event that is going to happen in a few months, or even a few days, may not carry much weight when they are faced with a real, live rival. So what you do after the baby arrives is probably even more important than the preliminary groundwork.

Maintain routines and rituals

A new baby in the house means big changes in lifestyle for your toddler or preschooler. As a way of protecting her against possible insecurity and anxiety, do your best to maintain the daily routines you followed before the baby arrived. Try to be patient with her insistence that things be done in a particular way — this may give her a sense of order and predictability in a world that, for her, has been turned upside down.

Involve your child

Without forcing it, do whatever you can to involve your first-born child as a helper in looking after the baby. If she seems interested, delegate special responsibilities to her, such as bringing in the baby's bath toys or winding up the music-box at naptime. It is particularly helpful to talk with her about what the baby is doing, what it might be feeling, and why it might be crying. Ask her for suggestions about what the baby might like or need, and make a big deal about any occasions when the baby smiles at or responds to her in some way. After all, it's hard to be hostile towards someone who needs your help, especially when they laugh at your jokes!

Highlight the differences

As you care for the baby, point out how grown-up your first-born is. For example, remind her that she can talk, eat all by herself, put on some clothes without help, while the baby still has to learn all of these things.

Create some 'special time'

Even though life is going to be very hectic with both of them to look after, try to keep some special, one-to-one time for your toddler each day during which you concentrate on her interests alone.

Be patient, but firm

Be as patient as you can in responding to any clinginess, defiance or tantrums, without giving in. You still need to set limits for acceptable behaviour, especially in regard to aggression shown towards the baby.

Listen to her feelings

The new baby's arrival may stir up strong negative feelings in your first-born. It probably sounds a bit like psychobabble, but try to respond to 'I hate the baby!' or 'I wish she'd never been born!' with something like: 'It sounds like you're really angry', rather than 'How dare you speak like that about your little sister!'. Accepting and acknowledging the negative feelings can help them to go away. Reacting defensively just adds fuel to the fire.

Rivalry in older children

Unfortunately, rivalry and hostility sometimes continue through to later years.

At this point, it's important to highlight the difference between the normal sibling squabbles that are daily occurrences in most families, and the types of conflicts that become bitter feuds. Because children are territorial, there will always be disputes about who owns what, who goes first, who gets to sit in the front seat, who gets the last chocolate biscuit, and so on. Most parents quickly develop a sixth sense about this, and try to be scrupulously fair about sharing out the goodies. Most parents also learn to let the tides of verbal bickering wash over them without paying too much attention, intervening only if there seems to be a threat to life or limb. If you always intervene in sibling squabbles you run the risk that children will manufacture situations and simulate emotions in order to gain attention and sympathy. A child can become skilled at playing the role of victim, thereby setting up their brother or sister for the undeserved label of 'villain'.

In some instances, normal territorial defensiveness evolves into something more like guerrilla warfare, with an underlying foundation of deep, mutual hostility. This often begins with one child complaining that the other always receives preferential treatment. She is not convinced by (or even interested in) detailed evidence showing that all goods and services have been distributed in precisely equal amounts.

Sometimes the child with the grievance does have a point. It is a fact of life that parents may feel more tenderly towards one child than another. Some children are, quite simply, easier to love. We are individuals before we are parents, and we have our own natural likes and dislikes. As our children grow, they each develop a unique personality, which we may find easy to live with or irritating. With the best will in the world, and despite strenuous effort, it is very hard to disguise those feelings, whether they are positive or negative. Because children are always on the lookout for signs of our approval or disapproval, they quickly pick up on any hints of favouritism. And so, the seeds of war are sown.

Deep resentment can also be created through natural feelings of jealousy if a brother or sister is more successful at school, is better looking, makes friends more easily, or is talented in a particular area, such as sport or music.

As with other wars, however, sometimes the original reason for the conflict becomes lost in the mists of time, and the battle is carried on simply through habit. If you have a feud going on in your family, it is probably not so important to work out how it started as it is to decide what to do about it. It is usually very difficult for the members of a family to sort out long-standing conflicts by themselves. Even if you sit down together and begin to discuss the subject calmly and reasonably, it generally doesn't take long before someone storms out of the room in tears, slamming the door behind them. Good listening skills are useful (see Chapter 18), and regular family meetings can help prevent a petty grievance from becoming an entrenched bitterness, but once this point has been reached, professional family counselling is probably the best option.

Parenting points

- There are many reasons why your first-born child may not be as happy about the arrival of your second as you are.
- Preparation for the baby's homecoming is useful, but probably not as important as what you do after she has taken up residence.
- Involve your first-born by recruiting her as your absolutely indispensable personal assistant.
- It is especially helpful to engage her in lots of discussion about what the baby is doing, what it might be feeling, and what it might like or need.
- Listen to any negative feelings that she may express about the baby, but set clear limits in regard to aggression. There are lots of excellent children's stories on this subject available from your library, which you can read with your first-born.
- Sibling squabbles in older children are a part of normal family life, but chronic feuding may require professional counselling.

PART FIVE
Born not made

12 Temperament and talent

Parents who have more than one child will almost certainly have been struck by the differences in traits, talents and temperament between their children. It is amazing how, with the same kind of upbringing, children can differ so much in their basic personality and abilities.

Nature and nurture

These differing characteristics strongly suggest that children's behaviour is a product not just of the influence and teaching of their parents, but of the combined effects of heredity and environment. Clearly, the unique personality profile of a child is partly the result of the efforts made to shape his development, but it is also due to tendencies that are simply part of his biological make-up.

Over the years there have been different schools of thought about this issue within the psychology profession. Some have laid strong emphasis on the influence of the family environment on the development of each child. In other words, it has been thought that the way parents respond to a child's behaviour, and the way family members relate to and interact with each other, are the most significant factors affecting behaviour. To some extent, this is true. Many of the ways in which children behave and develop are the direct result of parental teaching and influence. There is also no doubt that some behavioural problems result from family conflict, neglect or abuse, rather than from biological factors.

Biological 'givens'

However, the more I have worked with children, and attempted to help them and their families change some of the behaviours that cause stress and worry, the more I have become aware that there are significant biological 'givens' that make up each child's uniqueness. These 'givens' either cannot be modified, or can be changed only slightly after considerable effort and input, and include:

- intellectual capacity
- physical co-ordination
- proficiency and fluency with language
- preference for practical/outdoor activities
- sociability
- activity level
- temperament
- academic aptitude

If these characteristics were to be regarded as scales, most children would rate around the middle of the scale for each one. The children I deal with, however, tend to have an excess or deficit in some characteristic, which creates problems for their parents or teachers. Examples include intellectual disability, hyperactivity, extreme shyness, difficulty with anger management, and specific learning disability. In my experience it is almost always a case of accepting these characteristics as an aspect of a child's make-up, or as a tendency in his personality. The most practical approach is therefore to work around it, develop coping strategies, and modify it gradually, rather than trying to eliminate it.

If there are features of your child's behaviour that worry you or drive you crazy, consider whether these may be personality traits and therefore unlikely to change much despite your efforts. If they

are traits that bother you a lot, it may be that they clash with an aspect of your own personality. Examples of this kind of 'clash' include:
- shy child/outgoing parent
- bookworm child/sporty parent
- easygoing child/high-achieving parent
- boisterous child/quiet parent

Situations such as these call for acceptance and sensible compromise — however reluctant — rather than frustrating and futile attempts to achieve a personality transplant.

Baby personalities

Some of the clearest examples of the inborn nature of many traits have come from the work done with newborn babies, particularly by American paediatrician Dr T. Berry Brazelton. Dr Brazelton and his co-workers at Children's Hospital in Boston, USA, developed the Neonatal Behavioural Assessment Scale, which measures the responses of newborn babies on a number of different dimensions, including:
- degree of response to different kinds of stimulation
- speed of adaptation to repeated stimulation
- alertness
- motor maturity
- cuddliness
- consolability
- excitability
- activity levels
- stability of mood

Dr Brazelton's work has shown that there are clear behavioural differences between babies *only a few days old* on all these dimensions. When taken together, they add up to a distinct personality that is detectable and measurable virtually from birth.

As babies grow, their natural differences in temperament become more apparent. Some are remarkably easy to look after. They are usually happy and friendly, adapt easily to changes in their bodily state (such as hunger or temperature), are interested in the world around them, can be left to entertain themselves for quite long periods, and have regular feeding and sleeping cycles. Other babies are more difficult. They are usually irritable, react negatively to changes in bodily state, find it hard to settle into feeding and sleeping routines, and seem always to be crying.

Temperamentally 'easy' and 'difficult' babies are at opposite ends of a spectrum of baby personalities. These early tendencies are likely to persist to some degree throughout childhood. They will, of course, be modified by life experiences both within and outside the family, but in my experience the basic 'flavour' of a child's personality remains relatively constant. This has been confirmed by research, particularly in regard to characteristics such as:

- sociability
- activity level
- tendency to anxiety
- aggression
- 'stimulus seeking' (a preference for stimulation and excitement as opposed to quietness and predictability)

All of these traits have been shown to be enduring aspects of personality, recognisable in the early years and persisting into adulthood.

Abilities

Most people accept that children are born with natural aptitudes and potential in areas such as intellectual ability, physical co-ordination, artistic talent, and facility with language or mathematics. Natural talent usually shows itself by strong and early interest in particular activities — drawing, kicking a ball, playing with Lego, learning to read — and precocious development of skills in that area. Our job as parents is to watch for signs of interest and ability that might indicate a particular talent, then do what we can to encourage and foster it. On the other hand, sometimes our responsibility is to accept that our children lack ability or interest in areas that are important or dear to us, and not put pressure on them to achieve or perform if it is really beyond them.

Parenting points

- Even with the same upbringing, children differ in regard to basic personality and abilities.
- Children's behaviour is a product of the combined effects of heredity and environment.
- Differences in temperament can be clearly seen, even in newborn babies.
- Basic personality tendencies can be identified from an early age and may remain constant through childhood.
- Inborn temperament and tendencies can be modified somewhat, but generally they should be accepted and worked with, rather than trying to transform or transplant them.

13 Hyperactivity

Three-year-old Shane was referred to me by his family doctor because his parents were finding it extremely difficult to manage his behaviour. According to the doctor, they were 'at their wits' end', a phrase often used to describe the parents of such children.

When I visited Shane at home I could see why. As I rang the doorbell, a little boy raced down the hallway and used the glass panels on the front door to climb up to the handle. He wasn't able to undo the extra lock that had been fitted, but his mother wasn't far behind. With him tucked squirming under one arm, she opened the door with the other.

When I went inside, I recognised all of the signs of a house inhabited by a very active young child. There wasn't an ornament in sight, but there were broken toys scattered everywhere, creative little crayon additions to the wallpaper pattern, handprints and footprints in places that were hard to believe, and furniture that looked slightly the worse for wear.

We sat down in the lounge-room and Shane looked at me for a few seconds before climbing onto an armchair and bouncing on the seat. His mother told him to stop, but he carried on until she made a move towards him. He then quickly scrambled over the back of the chair onto the floor and ducked behind the couch. His mother and I had just begun talking when he ran towards the television and switched it on. 'No, Shane!', his mother said firmly. No response. Another threatening move and another dive for cover.

Shane's eighteen-month-old brother tottered into the room just as he was climbing onto the coffee table. Little brother thought this looked like fun and tried to clamber aboard. Shane pushed him off and he banged his head on the floor. Smiles from Shane, wails from little brother, angry threats from Mum.

Eventually, after many interruptions, I managed to get the story of Shane's lifestyle. He rose very early each morning and was in top gear from the moment he opened his eyes. Most activities held his attention only for a minute or two. Toys were lucky to last a few days in his hands before they fell apart. He was a fussy eater, not too keen on cuddles, and would throw major tantrums over minor frustrations. The daytime nap had long disappeared. The front and back doors had to be locked in case he made a run for it.

Shane seemed to have no sense of danger, little sensitivity to pain, and a mission to climb literally anything. He was quite happy to go to sleep, but would wake at least twice a night and come to his parents' bed. No wonder his parents were at their wits' end. Shane appeared to be genuinely hyperactive.

What is hyperactivity?

All toddlers are programmed to be busy, energetic explorers, but some are a lot busier than others. Some just potter about quietly and happily, most are quite energetic and determined, and a small percentage (almost always boys) are *very* active indeed. For this small group of toddler tornadoes, and of older children, the word 'hyperactive' is often used.

But what is the difference between a very active and a hyperactive child? This is not easy to answer and many child-health professionals are therefore cautious about using the term 'hyperactive'. Although there is a recognised disorder commonly known as hyperactivity, it shares characteristics with other disorders, such as developmental delay, and overlaps with the extremes of normal behaviour. This can make it difficult to identify accurately and definitively.

True hyperactivity has the following four main features:
1 The child shows *very high levels of activity*, as if he is driven by some kind of internal motor that never runs out of gas.
2 He seems *unable to concentrate* on a task for very long and is easily distracted.
3 He is *very impulsive*, and may do silly or dangerous things without any thought for the consequences.
4 He has a *very low tolerance for frustration*: small irritations can lead to big explosions!

These behavioural features are present from an early age and usually become obvious in toddlerhood. Some parents say that their child was noticeably different from birth. Quite a few have told me how alert their child seemed very shortly after birth, and several have used the striking expression: 'He was so alert and wide-eyed, he looked as if he had been here before'.

Attention deficit disorder (ADD)

Over recent years, some researchers have come to believe that the inability to attend and concentrate is the main feature of hyperactivity, leading them to rename it Attention Deficit Disorder or ADD. The logic is that the child buzzes around not because his accelerator pedal is stuck, but because he is simply unable to concentrate on anything for very long, and so is constantly seeking new stimulation. Regardless of the cause, however, it is certainly the very high activity level that parents notice and have difficulty coping with.

Although the term ADD has now replaced 'hyperactivity', strictly speaking this is not quite accurate. The term ADD should be reserved to describe those children whose primary problem is one of attention deficit. There are some children who have a short attention span, are easily distracted, have difficulty following instructions, may often seem lost in a world of their own, and are very disorganised, but who do not seem to be hyperactive. These children, who appear to have a genuine attention deficit, have a proprietary right to the ADD label. Children who have all the features of attention deficit, together with hyperactivity (and these are much more common), are more accurately described as having Attention Deficit Hyperactivity Disorder or ADHD. It is the hyperactivity of these children that captures everybody else's attention, even though their own may be slightly lacking.

So, even though ADD seems to be the most popular way of describing hyperactive children, I prefer to use the more accurate term ADHD.

Main features

While this is not a formal checklist, some of the most common presenting features of ADHD are:

- *Always on the go*. Very active from an early age.
- *Sleeping problems*. Has trouble getting to sleep, and may wake early.
- *Can't sit still*. Is often fidgety and restless.
- *Short attention span*. Moves quickly from one activity to another.
- *Excitable*. Is very easily 'hyped up'. The company of other children quickly leads to silly and outrageous behaviour.
- *Impulsive*. Does potentially dangerous things without thinking of the consequences, such as climbing high trees or riding a bicycle or skateboard 'to the max'. A thrill seeker.
- *Easily frustrated*. Has a very low frustration tolerance. Even minor frustrations can lead to major tantrums.
- *Reacts badly to change*. Changes in routine, or of environment or caregiver, can provoke unsettled behaviour.
- *Bossy*. Wants things his own way all the time. Doesn't like taking turns in games.
- *Moody*. Moods may change quickly and dramatically. May cry easily.
- *Demanding*. Has an advanced diploma in nagging. May talk constantly.
- *Being male*. Most ADHD children are boys.

Not all cases will exhibit all of these features. As with all children, every hyperactive child is unique, with his own pattern of characteristics. There is, nevertheless, enough of a similarity in the development and typical behaviour patterns of these children to allow them to be grouped together and given a name.

Additional features

Parents of ADHD children sometimes remark that their child appears socially immature, seeming to have difficulty getting on with other children and having no real friends. When an ADHD child gets together with other children, he becomes silly and over-excited, and his playmates soon become tired of this. Add in the bossiness, unwillingness to take turns, and low frustration tolerance and it is easy to see why ADHD children can be socially isolated.

Another feature often associated with ADHD is specific learning disability or, as it is more commonly known, 'dyslexia' (see Chapter 14). There seems to be a link between the two disorders, which is stronger than you would expect on the basis of chance. Even taking concentration and behavioural problems into account, some ADHD children have extra difficulties with learning to read and write, which suggests some kind of neurological 'block'.

Some writers have suggested that ADHD children are more likely to be clumsy and poorly co-ordinated than other children, but my experience has tended to be the opposite. Perhaps as a kind of compensation for their other difficulties, the ADHD children that I have seen are often gifted with excellent physical co-ordination and strength.

ADHD children are often described as 'attention seeking', which I don't think is an accurate interpretation of their behaviour. Some children do hunger for the spotlight, but genuine ADHD children attract the attention of parents and teachers without conscious intent. ADHD children can't be ignored, but this does not mean that they seek attention for its own sake.

Diagnosing ADHD

If you feel that your child may have ADHD, talk to your family doctor, who will be able to refer you to someone who will be able to confirm the diagnosis, probably a paediatrician or a child psychiatrist.

Unfortunately, there is no absolute diagnosis for ADHD. It is usually done on the basis of developmental history, parent reports, school reports, and standardised rating scales. Some clinics use sophisticated brainwave analysis, but even this can only add to the probability that it is ADHD, rather than confirm the diagnosis absolutely. It would be good to have a measurable blood test, or something we could point to on a scan and say authoritatively, 'There it is!', but regrettably we are not yet at that stage. It is lack of certainty in diagnosis that has caused some professionals to be sceptical about the existence of ADHD, which is discouraging and frustrating for the many parents who fight for recognition that their children's problems are not due to 'bad parenting', as has so often been suggested or implied.

Coping in the preschool years

Whether or not a diagnosis of hyperactivity is confirmed, parents need to learn strategies to help them cope with their child's behaviour — not only to help the child, but also to make sure they don't go under themselves.

Day after day of acting as minder for a turbo toddler, dealing with an endless stream of demands, tantrums and dangerous antics, can leave a parent driven to the point of exhausted desperation.

The first step back to sanity is *acceptance*. It is important to accept that this is the way your child is, and that there is no quick fix for the problems he presents. It might sound extreme, but genuine hyperactivity is a bit like a physical disability. Just as parents of children with a physical disability need to come to terms with their child's problem and realise that they will have to adjust their lifestyle and expectations accordingly, so too do parents of ADHD children.

The second step is *not to blame yourself* for your child's behaviour, or punish yourself by constantly asking 'What have I done wrong?'. You may sometimes get the impression from relatives and friends that they believe it is somehow all your fault, and that if you were just a bit firmer or more consistent the problems would disappear. As the parent of an ADHD child, you know how hard you have to work just to keep your head above water, and that the usual methods just don't seem to work. You certainly don't need to be made to feel guilty as well.

The third step is to get yourself a *support network*. You cannot look after a hyperactive toddler or preschooler seven days a week for months on end without a break. As the main caregiver, you need to have your partner give you a spell every day, even if it's only to sit down with the newspaper and a cup of tea for half an hour while the bath and bedtime routine is underway. A morning or an afternoon to yourself once a week while nanna, an aunty or a friend puts on a crash helmet and takes over is also not too much to ask. Daycare can be a lifesaver, especially if you don't have family living nearby. Good daycare not only provides a much-needed break for you, but also a wide range of activities and equipment to keep your child busy — and it may even tire him out a little!

Adapting the home front

Once you have accepted your child for who he is, switched off your guilt button, and got your support network in place, turn your attention to the home front.

Childproofing your house

In the early years, reduce the opportunity for disasters and dangerous accidents by childproofing your house. Remove all ornaments and precious breakables, fit childproof locks to cupboards containing dangerous temptations, and don't invest in new furniture or carpets for the moment. In general, try to reduce as much as you can the chances of your child breaking something or being hurt. You will have enough to do without putting yourself under any unnecessary stress. Sacrificing decor for sanity can be a wise trade-off.

Routines

Establish a good routine. A structured schedule of activities can be very helpful in coping with a hyperactive toddler or preschooler. Even more than an average child, an ADHD child needs to be kept busy, so plan a daily programme with variety and changes of scene. A daily routine can calm children and give them a sense of security. Even the way you do things can be important. Slight changes of routine, such as using the wrong colour cup or sitting in a different seat, can produce storms of protest. It is much easier to go along with rituals like this than cause trouble by insisting that he is 'being silly' or that it doesn't matter. It might not matter to you, but it obviously does to him.

Outdoor activities

Your child will probably hunger for outdoor activities such as running, climbing, kicking a ball and general exploring. You may well find that spending some time outside each day will become essential for both of you, partly because he will enjoy it so much and partly because the energy he burns up may mean an earlier bedtime or a more peaceful night for you.

Daycare and preschool

A busy daily programme is important for very active children, and preschools and daycare centres can be helpful in providing this. Very few families can afford to set up their homes like a kindergarten, with a huge range of child-centred toys, activities and resources. Also, professional childcare staff can be relaxed, patient and attentive with your child when you can't because you are simply worn out. You may be aware that because your patience and energy have been stretched to the limit, you no longer enjoy playing with your child, even though you know how important it is for his development. Professional childcare can lift some of that worry from your shoulders.

When push meets shove

As a general rule, I think it is important to try to modify your lifestyle and expectations as much as possible to cater for your hyperactive child's special needs. But there will still be times when confrontations cannot be avoided. In order to keep these to a minimum, pick your fights carefully. Think before you say 'No!'. Save your energy for big battles such as personal safety, aggression towards others, damage to property, bathtime, and bedtime. These will keep you busy enough, so try not to worry about the smaller things sich as tidiness, manners or sharing toys. Let as much as you can flow over you, but when the issue is important, hang in there until you win. Here are some strategies that may be helpful:

- *Set priorities*. Decide which behaviours are important to you and which are not. Concentrate on those that upset or affect you most, and work to keep the lid on them.
- *Give one warning, then act*. Children soon learn to ignore a stream of warnings and threats that aren't followed up. Always give one clear warning, then follow through with action. It is best to talk less and act more.
- *Time-out*. For serious misbehaviour that you cannot accept, you can remove your child from the family routine for a set period (see Chapter 8).

Monitoring diet

Some parents have found that their child's misbehaviour gets worse after he has had certain fizzy drinks, sweets or snack foods. Eliminating these things from his diet may lead to some improvement — trial and error will guide you here. Allergic reactions to certain foods seem to be associated with hyperactivity episodes in some children. If you think this may be the case with your child, discuss it with your family doctor.

ADHD and the school-aged child

During the primary-school years, the hyperactive child's behaviour gradually changes. Full-on, flat-out hyperactivity eases back a notch or two to become restlessness and fidgetiness. While the characteristic short attention span, distractibility, impulsiveness and short fuse remain, they do become less extreme. Unfortunately, despite this gradual improvement, these years are certain to cause a few headaches because the education system seems to highlight all of the hyperactive child's difficulties.

If people had set out to design an environment that would emphasise the negative features of ADHD in the most dramatic way, they would have designed a school. Our education system requires children to sit still, be quiet, listen to instructions, and do as they are told for several hours every day. These are all precisely the things that ADHD children find intrinsically difficult. So it is no surprise that they are constantly in trouble for fidgeting, being out of their seats, calling out, not finishing their work, not paying attention, disturbing their classmates, staring out the window, losing their equipment, and 'answering back'.

Regardless of whether your child's teachers accept the existence of such a thing as ADHD, the very nature of his behaviour will demand specialist input and support. This will probably come from a school psychologist, who will devise an appropriate behavioural programme. Any associated learning difficulties will need to be assessed and dealt with as well.

Behaviour management at school

It will be very much easier if everyone who is working with an ADHD child accepts at least the *possibility* of ADHD as the cause of his problems. ADHD children are not maliciously or wilfully naughty — they simply can't help themselves. Because of the nature of their difficulties, it is not realistic to expect them to behave at all times as other children do. Some allowance must be made for their distractibility, short attention span, low frustration tolerance, impulsiveness, and so on. Teachers who accept the existence of ADHD, and have some knowledge of its effects on classroom behaviour, will be more likely and willing to adjust their programme to cater for the ADHD child's needs.

It is always difficult for teachers to cater for individual needs in a classroom of thirty-plus pupils. There are a few basic strategies, however, that can help ADHD children conform to classroom expectations:

- *Keep instructions brief.* The short attention span of ADHD children makes it difficult for them to follow long or complicated instructions. Try to break them down into a sequence of clear, simple steps. Use brief, written memory-aids where possible.
- *Break down tasks into manageable 'chunks'.* ADHD children are much more likely to complete a task if it is presented as a series of mini-goals. This is particularly important on larger, more complex tasks, such as social studies projects, but can even be helpful with simple maths and English exercises: 'Okay, Shane, I'll be back in five minutes to see how you have gone on the first three of those problems'.
- *Strategic placement.* It's quite easy to spot the ADHD child in a classroom. He's the one who will be asked to sit right by the teacher's knees when she is reading a story, whose desk will be right next to the teacher's, or whose desk will be isolated in a corner when the other children's desks are in groups. These are all sensible strategies for ensuring that ADHD children stay on task, and should not be regarded as punishments. The attention of the ADHD child often needs to be brought back into focus, and it is much easier to do this if the teacher is close by. Similarly, ADHD children often don't work well in a group situation, and isolating them actually helps them to get on with the job.
- *Self-control.* ADHD children, more so than other children, need external guidance to help them manage their behaviour, but as they grow older they can be taught to be more aware of the problems that their distractibility, impulsiveness and restlessness can cause for them. They can also learn 'self-talk' methods that will help them to control their own behaviour, rather than being reliant on teacher-mediated instructions, rewards and punishments. With self-talk, your child learns literally to instruct, coach, and encourage himself to use strategies and follow procedures that other children use automatically and unconsciously. Teaching a child to use self-talk is very simple, but ongoing practice is necessary for the technique to be effective. A school or child psychologist will be able to teach your child these strategies from about the age of seven years.

- *Routine.* Most ADHD children tend to become unsettled and overexcited by changes of routine and teacher. Structure, sameness, and predictability seem to reduce the chances of problem behaviour occurring.
- *Praise.* Because ADHD children are so often in trouble for not following instructions, not completing work, calling out, acting impulsively, and so on, it is not surprising that their self-image can become very negative. They never seem to be able to do anything right, and can begin to see themselves as just plain 'bad'. As they become older, they may begin to feel that there is no point in making an effort, and that they might as well live up to their labels. To stop this negative cycle, it is important for teachers always to be on the lookout for good behaviour, and to acknowledge it with a word of praise, a sticker, or a certificate. Also, the parents of ADHD children can feel as battered and despondent as their offspring, and a little good news from school now and then can mean as much to them as to their child.

Behaviour management at home

During the primary-school years, parents are at least able to share the day-to-day burden of looking after their ADHD child with his teachers. Also, with luck, the hurricane levels of hyperactivity will have eased back a degree or two. However, the problems of impulsiveness, short fuse, mood swings, low boredom threshold, short attention span (except for video games) will remain. Try to use the same behaviour-management strategies that applied during the preschool years:

- *Acceptance of the problem.* Adjust your expectations to take account of your child's behavioural disability.
- *Eliminate guilt.* Don't be hard on yourself or plague yourself with questions such as 'Where did we go wrong?'. It's not your fault.
- *Keep him busy.* A busy programme of after-school and weekend activities will reduce the possibility of mischievous escapades

and of your hyperactive child driving the rest of the family mad with nagging and noisiness.
- *Keep things structured.* This applies not only to daily routines, but also to rules. You will have to be much more *persistent, consistent,* and *insistent* in regard to rules than you would like to be. ADHD children are reliant on externally imposed discipline to help them manage their behaviour, until they are able to learn self-control strategies. So for everyone's sake, you will have to be more of a sergeant major than you would like to be.
- *Save your energy for the big battles.* Keep rules to a minimum, but make sure that they are observed. When a battle is necessary, make sure you win.
- *Be on the lookout for good behaviour.* Just as in school, it is possible for your interactions with your child at home to become very negative, with the same kind of consequences. To avoid this, try to recognise and acknowledge examples of co-operative, helpful, and thoughtful behaviour, however small they may be.

Medication and ADHD

For some reason not yet completely understood, stimulant medication can have a dramatic effect on the symptoms of ADHD. Many children with all the classic signs of ADHD, from early school-age through to teenagers, have been helped dramatically by it. In school they can attend and concentrate better, are much less fidgety and disruptive, and are noticeably more able to complete tasks and assignments. Sometimes even their handwriting and work presentation improves. At home they may seem calmer, less irritable, and less inclined to fly off the handle.

It is thought that ADHD children may have a neurochemical imbalance in their brains that causes their behavioural problems. It is possible that stimulant medication somehow restores the balance, and enables those parts of the brain that control attention and planning to function more effectively. It does not act as a sedative, and its effect is certainly not 'mind bending' as it is sometimes described. Although I am convinced of the benefits of medication for children whose lives have been made miserable by ADHD, it does not work for all children, and there are some side-effects that need to be considered. And remember that even if medication is effective, some form of behavioural programme is almost always necessary as well. You can obtain further information about drug treatment from your family doctor, or from one of the many books written about ADHD.

The long-term outlook

Be prepared for the fact that the core features of ADHD usually do not disappear over time, even though they may moderate a little. ADHD is an inherent part of a child's personality, and basic personality traits tend to remain constant. Your child may learn to control his behaviour more effectively as he matures, but the tendency towards restlessness, distractibility, and impulsiveness can persist even through to adulthood.

Parenting points

- ADHD is known by different names, including 'hyperactivity' and 'ADD'.
- ADHD has four main features: very high levels of activity; short attention span; impulsiveness; and low frustration tolerance. These features have to have been present from an early age.
- True ADD is different from ADHD because it lacks the feature of hyperactivity.
- ADHD is probably most difficult to manage in the toddler and preschool years, but a well thought out battle plan can help you to survive.
- School and ADHD don't mix very well. It is possible to cater for an ADHD child's special needs provided that teachers accept the true nature of the problem and are prepared to accommodate the child's differences.

- ADHD and specific learning disability are often associated, but they are not two sides of the same coin.
- At home, a clear and consistently enforced set of rules will help you to survive the primary-school years, but it is a good idea to seek professional guidance.
- Stimulant medication can dramatically alleviate the symptoms of ADHD in some children.
- The core features of ADHD are likely to persist through childhood and adolescence, and in some cases may remain as personality tendencies even into adulthood.
- Associations of parents of ADHD children operate in most major centres and are valuable sources of information and support.

14 Specific learning disability

Matthew's parents had high hopes for him when he started school. As a toddler and preschooler his language development had been somewhat slow, and he had not really begun talking in sentences until he was over three, but his language skills were now good. He seemed bright, alert, and interested in his environment. His preschool teacher had been a little concerned that just before he turned five he was still having trouble writing his name independently, was still confusing some colour names, and that his drawings were quite immature, but sometimes boys did seem to lag a little behind in these areas. Matthew had not been particularly interested in the indoor preschool activities such as drawing, painting, doing puzzles and listening to stories — he much preferred to be outdoors climbing over the play equipment, digging in the sandpit, and racing around with his friends.

When Matthew started school his progress with reading and writing was very slow. His handwriting was big and clumsy, he often reversed his letters, and he had major problems in learning to spell. The words he learned in reading one day were forgotten the next. He would bring the same book home so often that he knew each page by heart. He seemed to have particular trouble with small, frequently occurring words like 'and', 'the', 'for', 'was', but could remember 'helicopter' and 'hippopotamus'. His oral language skills were good, and he was quick to pick up new concepts in maths.

By the end of Matthew's second year at school, despite extra one-to-one support, the gap between him and his classmates had widened. He was becoming discouraged, and had begun to say things such as 'I'll never learn to read' and 'I'm dumb'. Eventually the school psychologist was called in to assess Matthew's intelligence, which turned out to be slightly above average. It was becoming clear that Matthew in fact had a specific learning disability (LD).

What is a specific learning disability?

One way to explain specific learning disability is to describe what *doesn't* cause it. It refers to a difficulty in learning that is *not* caused by below-average intelligence, inadequate teaching, perceptual difficulties, or emotional problems. If a child is of average intellectual ability, has received good teaching, has no vision or hearing problems, has no major emotional problems that might be affecting his learning or motivation, and is still having difficulty learning to read and write, there is a good chance that he or she might be learning disabled.

A specific learning disability is therefore not the same as learning difficulties caused by overall below-average intelligence. In fact, the simplest way to describe LD is as an innate difficulty in learning to read and write despite normal intelligence.

Other pointers to the possibility of a specific learning disability are:
- being male (most learning-disabled youngsters are boys)
- language delay in the toddler and preschool years
- great difficulty in retaining reading vocabulary, despite frequent repetition
- significant slowness in learning to write
- persistently clumsy handwriting
- persistent letter reversal past the first year of school
- frequent inversion of letter order ('siad' for 'said')
- immature drawing skills

LD and ADHD

There is also a reasonably high correlation between LD and ADHD, which is characterised by a short attention span, impulsiveness and constant motion (see Chapter 13). Some child-health professionals working in this field tend to talk about LD and ADHD as two sides of the same coin. In my opinion, although the two often occur together, they are not necessarily linked.

Dyslexia

The term 'dyslexia' is often used as an alternative to specific learning disability, but the two don't actually mean the same thing. Strictly speaking, dyslexia refers to an inability to read, or difficulty with reading. It is very rare for a child with a learning disability to have isolated reading problems without an associated difficulty with writing and spelling. One can be more severe than the other, but the two usually go hand in hand. Even so, it looks like the use of 'dyslexia' as a shorthand term for specific learning disability may be here to stay.

What causes LD?

Because the signs of LD are present from the preschool years, it seems reasonable to conclude that it must be innate. We are all born with a unique profile of talents, aptitudes and weaknesses, and it seems that this also applies to the ability to read and write.

Reading and writing involve a complex set of perceptual and intellectual processes. It is quite possible that, despite average intelligence, some children do not have the required neurological 'equipment' necessary for them to acquire literacy skills easily. It may be that for some reason, as yet unknown, those parts of the brain involved in learning to read and write work differently in some children. We readily accept, for example, individual differences in artistic talent, mathematical ability, and a whole range of other skills. Why shouldn't the same apply to reading and writing?

What can be done to help?

Working with learning-disabled children has been a special interest of mine for several years. Helping these children requires a great deal of patience, flexibility, persistence, and teamwork from all concerned — parents, teachers, special educators, and the children themselves.

The first step is *acceptance* of the possibility of LD. Unfortunately, not all educators are equally aware or accepting of the existence of LD, and learning-disabled children can sometimes be unfairly labelled as lazy, or inaccurately labelled as unintelligent.

The second step is *assessment*. If you feel that your child might have a learning disability you can request an assessment through the school psychologist. Although there is no doubt that the signs of LD can be present earlier, in my opinion the best time to look closely at the possibility of LD is after a child has been at school for about one year. Before this, even if a child is clearly not making the academic progress that would be expected on the basis of his obviously normal intelligence, most teachers are inclined to be optimistic. They will reassure parents that some children are late developers academically, and that it is far too early to start worrying. Unfortunately, this optimism often proves to be ill-founded.

The picture can become blurred if a child exhibits features of ADHD as well. If a child is restless, inattentive, and has a short attention span, it is easy to conclude that this is why he is not acquiring literacy skills. There is clearly some truth in this interpretation, but in my experience it is the learning disability that is the core problem, not the lack of attention to task. Of course, the two factors do interact. If a child has genuine and ongoing difficulty with a task, as LD children do with reading and writing, he will naturally tend to avoid doing it. If the amount of time he spends engaged in academic work is already below par because of his short attention span, and this is compounded by task avoidance, the scene is clearly set for a descending spiral of poor performance. The descent is accelerated by the sense of failure the child experiences when he compares his own progress with that of his classmates. The final ingredients in this toxic mixture are the feelings of despair and discouragement that LD children often experience as they struggle to master the skills that seem to come so easily to other children.

So, there clearly are a number of factors that can delay or obscure the accurate diagnosis of LD, especially in the first years of school.

How is LD assessed?

Once it becomes clearer that a child's lack of progress in reading and writing might be due to LD, a more thorough assessment will probably be carried out. This can include a general intellectual (IQ) assessment, and possibly an assessment of some of the specific perceptual and psychological processes that are thought to be involved in the complex business of learning to read and write. These can include things such as auditory perception, phonological awareness, auditory short-term memory, visual discrimination, visual memory, sequencing, and motor co-ordination.

Vision and hearing tests should be carried out as a matter of course, as should a detailed analysis of the child's current academic skills and learning strategies.

In my opinion there is a risk, however odd it may sound, of having too many test results and more information than can be usefully applied to a practical remedial programme. Questions that should be asked before any assessment is done include: 'What is the purpose of this test? What information will it give us? How can the results be used in a practical way?'. There is a danger that the exhaustive assessment of LD may provide pages of indigestible test results that have little practical relevance to helping children improve their reading and writing skills. Some researchers believe that the most effective remedy for lack of progress in reading and writing, whether caused by LD or not, is simply lots of practice under the guidance of a skilled and sympathetic teacher. By implication, complex batteries of tests are unnecessary.

In my opinion, the most useful assessment information includes:
- a detailed analysis of current academic skills and learning strategies;
- results of an IQ test; and
- an indication of whether a child's primary learning 'channel' is auditory or visual.

What do LD children need?

Current techniques in the teaching of reading and writing have moved a long way from those used a generation ago, which were based on the 'building block' method of breaking words down into their component sounds. Words with simple, easily learnt letter combinations were taught first and drilled repetitively. Early reading texts were based on this simple vocabulary and were therefore rather boring and meaningless ('The cat sat on the mat'). Spelling was taught in a similar, cumulative way, building from simple to complex, and emphasising 'word families' — groups of words containing similar sounds. These methods, although effective, could be rather dull and tedious, especially in the early stages of learning to read.

Over the last twenty years, the emphasis in the teaching of reading has switched from analysing words into their component sounds and building simple sentences from basic vocabulary, to providing the beginning reader with vibrant, interesting texts and an emphasis on reading for meaning. The philosophy behind this approach is that children who are motivated to read material because it is interesting will learn to identify and remember new words without having to be drilled in the component sounds beforehand. By constant exposure to new material they will, with guidance and support, learn to recognise recurring patterns of letters and thereby learn the regularities of written language. In this way, they will naturally extend their reading and writing vocabulary without the need for formal, repetitive teaching. This approach relies on children's natural problem-solving abilities, such as their ability to notice and identify recurring patterns of letters as they are exposed to new vocabulary. Children are then able to match these patterns of symbols to their store of knowledge about the world and to their own experiences, and in this way the words they learn acquire meaning.

Similarly, the emphasis in teaching the skills of writing is now on encouraging children to write about their own experiences, rather than restricting them to generating simple sentences within the limitations of a sterile, basic vocabulary. Also, rather than waiting to work through the levels of a formal spelling programme, children have been encouraged to experiment with whatever knowledge they may have of sound–letter associations and to invent the spelling of words they don't yet know. Spelling lists are based on the child's current interests and needs, rather than on word families that may have no relevance to current work.

These methods generally work well for most children. Unfortunately, they are not helpful for children with LD. Learning-disabled children require much more drilling and repetition of the basic components of reading and writing, and are likely to benefit from traditional, step-by-step, phonic-based methods of teaching. They also benefit from the use of all sensory modalities — sound, touch, movement, colour, shape, rhyme, song — which helps newly learnt material to 'stick'. The rationale is that by using many different paths to learning, it may be possible to detour around the 'roadblock'.

Children with LD also require different expectations in regard to quantity and type of work output. It needs to be recognised that it can take as much or more effort for an LD child to produce two sentences as it does for another child to produce two pages of work. And if an orally skilled child has to sweat to produce one paragraph of misspelt, badly constructed sentences, why not allow him the freedom to record his stories or assignments on tape? Instead of having to write pages on a project, why not suggest labelled diagrams, three dimensional models, an oral presentation, or a combination of all three?

A word processor can liberate LD children from the stress and frustration of constantly producing untidy work, and can be a real boon for those who struggle with accurate letter formations.

A learning-disabled child is a challenge to a teacher's patience, flexibility and creativity, the challenge being to enable the child to learn and express his learning without a constant sense of frustration and failure. Acquiring and retaining literacy skills is difficult for LD children, and it is not uncommon for everyone involved to become impatient and frustrated at their slow progress. Because the self-esteem of LD children takes a consistent battering at school, always look for and encourage other areas of strength and achievement in their lives to balance the frustration and hurt they can experience.

Finally, because LD is so resistant to treatment, there is a wide range of 'alternative' therapies available, such as coloured lenses, rhythmic body movements, and manipulation of the skull. Before spending your money on these remedies, I urge you to consult an experienced school psychologist or paediatrician to discuss their scientific credibility and chances of success.

Parenting points

- Specific learning disability (LD) is an innate difficulty in learning to read and write, despite normal intelligence. Its cause is unknown.
- Not all educators acknowledge the existence or importance of LD.
- The signs of LD are probably present in the kindergarten years, but do not become obvious until a child has been at school for a year or so.
- LD and ADHD often occur together, which makes early diagnosis more difficult.
- Complex assessment procedures are available to assist in the diagnosis of LD, but these do not always lead to effective intervention strategies.
- Current teaching philosophies and practices are not helpful for LD children, who benefit from more traditional teaching methods.
- Acquiring literacy skills is a long, hard and painful process for LD children, and their self-esteem can be very much at risk.
- Teachers of LD children need to be creative, flexible and extremely patient, as do their parents.

PART SIX
Gender and sexuality

15 Girls and boys

From the moment of birth, our gender is an important part of our identity. In fact, it's likely that the very first words spoken about us were those that told our parents whether they had a girl or a boy. And now, with the use of ultrasound scanners, some parents know the sex of their child even before the birth.

Now, when parents make decisions about the kinds of clothes or toys to buy their son or daughter, or what colour to paint the nursery, they are more aware of the implications of the customs associated with gender. In societies across the world, and throughout history, there have been clear differences in the ways in which women and men, girls and boys, have been expected to behave. In recent decades, the feminist movement has made us more aware that some of our beliefs about differences between the sexes are based on custom rather than biology. If this is so, then our beliefs and expectations can and should be changed, especially if the lives of girls and boys are being influenced negatively by society's attitudes.

How many of the differences in behaviour between girls and boys are influenced by genetics, and how many are shaped by custom and teaching? Do girls and boys act as they do because parents and other adults encourage and teach them to behave in gender-stereotyped ways, or is there also some biological influence at work?

Biology and learning

There is no doubt that social influences can be powerful. Some of these are subtle, some are very obvious: 'Don't climb that tree — you'll tear your dress' or 'Don't be such a sissy — boys don't cry'. Some interesting experiments have shown that adults behave in markedly different ways towards the same child, depending on whether the child is dressed as a girl or a boy.

But that's not the whole story. Research in developmental psychology confirms some significant differences between the sexes, some of which seem to be biologically based. For example, girls learn to talk sooner than boys, and boys are much more likely to develop speech and language problems. Girls are quicker to toilet train. Boys are much more likely to have behavioural problems at school, to have difficulty learning to read, and to be diagnosed as learning disabled or hyperactive. From an early age girls tend to show more sympathy towards other children in distress, and are more nurturing to younger children. They are also usually more compliant than boys. Some researchers have even reported the possibility of structural differences between the brains of males and females, which could be related to the skills at which boys and girls excel: verbal for girls and mathematical-spatial for boys.

The human species is the product of millions of years of evolution. In other species, there are clear male–female behavioural differences that accompany the physical differences, and it is possible that some of the behavioural differences between women and men are partly the product of physical and behavioural evolution.

So it seems likely that biology and learning, heredity and environment, each play a part in explaining why girls and boys behave in the ways they do. Some aspects of their behaviour may be 'wired in', while others are the result of social conditioning.

Children are individuals

So how do we know which is which? Part of the answer lies in knowing your child as an individual. Each child is born with a unique profile of strengths and talents. Each seems to have natural aptitude for some tasks, which are picked up quickly and easily, while other skills may take much effort and practice to acquire. Some children have excellent physical co-ordination and enjoy running, climbing and riding. Others show particular talent and interest in drawing, music, or construction-type activities. Some children have excellent verbal skills from an early age, which is often associated with the easy acquisition of reading and writing skills. And, of course, in all these examples, the opposite may also be true.

An important part of our job as parents is to be aware of our children's individual patterns of skills and abilities and to try to develop these, regardless of whether they fit traditional gender stereotypes. If your daughter shows talent in kicking a ball, give her a chance to play soccer. If your son shows an interest in dance, enrol him in a local class. Don't close doors to your child on the basis of sex-role prejudice.

Sex-role conditioning

It's also important to be aware of the subtle and even unconscious ways in which we maintain the undesirable aspects of sex-role stereotypes. Boys need the opportunity to express their feelings and be nurturing. Girls need the chance to play rough-and-tumble games, and to bang nails into wood. Even if girls and boys do have natural tendencies to behave in certain ways, they don't *have* to — they can be encouraged to develop non-stereotyped ways of acting, thinking and being.

This is especially important in the field of education. For example, preschool teachers are in a good position to counter some of the expectations we have about the way girls and boys play. Girls can be encouraged to spend time at the woodwork table or building with blocks. Boys can be enticed to the dress-up corner if there is a choice of suitable clothes for them. Because preschoolers sometimes actively exclude children of the opposite sex from their preferred games, it may be necessary to have girls-only or boys-only times for certain activities.

Once children get to school age, there is a large amount of research evidence to show that boys tend to dominate classroom life. They are louder, more assertive, and more disruptive, and for all these reasons capture more than their fair share of teacher attention. This feature is so marked that even when teachers are made aware of its effects, and attempt to compensate for it, they often still find it difficult to give equal attention to girls.

Schools are now becoming much more aware of the ways in which gender stereotypes can be unconsciously reinforced through the use of sexist language, subject choice, career options, and unthinking assumptions about what girls and boys are able to do. And we, as parents, should too.

Parenting points

- Some gender differences are based more on tradition and custom than biology.
- As parents we need to be aware of the potentially negative effects of sexual stereotyping.
- The safest path to take is to know your child as an individual, and to be aware of her unique profile of strengths and talents.
- Nurture your child's natural aptitudes, regardless of whether this fits traditional gender stereotypes. This is especially important in the field of education.

16 Sexual behaviour

Imagine walking into your four-year-old daughter's room to find her and her little boyfriend with their pants down showing each other their genitals. How do you respond? Do you excuse yourself and walk out? Do you scold them? Do you carry on about your business and pretend that nothing out of the ordinary is happening? Or is this a golden opportunity for some sex education?

Early sexual behaviour

There is no doubt that some degree of sexual behaviour is normal in children from as young as two years of age. It is common for toddlers and preschoolers to display an interest in their own and others' genitals. This is partly due to a natural sense of exploration, as children find out more about themselves and their world, but children do seem to be particularly aware of those parts of their body that one day will have a sexual function.

Young children usually show their sexual interest and sensitivity by displaying and touching their own bodies. They may take delight in running around naked, or standing in such a way as to show off their genitals to maximum effect. They may bend over and peer at their bottoms, poke at or waggle themselves (according to gender), or perform little dances that call attention to their genitals. Not surprisingly, it is in the bath, while dressing, and when swimming that these behaviours are most likely to occur. They are usually accompanied by lots of laughing, giggling and silly noises, and are quite clearly performed as a kind of game. There is nothing secret about these behaviours, and in fact making them very public (within the family) constitutes most of the fun.

From self to others

As children reach the preschool years, they become more aware of and interested in the bodies of other children and adults. Rather than just enjoying the slightly wicked game of showing themselves off, they become more curious about what other people's bodies look like, and will take any opportunity to look at other children's genitals, or at adults' naked bodies. Once their curiosity is aroused, they may try to touch as well as look, and this can include touching their mother's or other women's breasts. Just as with the streaking and flashing, these behaviours are usually accompanied by knowing giggles, and it seems that the child is playing a game that she realises is pushing the limits of acceptability.

Research has shown that up to the age of five or six years, more obviously sexual behaviours such as masturbation are much less common than just looking and touching. While one study suggests that half to two-thirds of young children will show interest in their own and others' genitals in some way, no more than a quarter of them are likely to masturbate (more boys than girls), and only a very small percentage will display the behaviours that adults use to express their sexuality, such as imitation of intercourse.

Secret games

In the early school years, children move on to the next stage of their sexual development, which involves the same kinds of looking and touching behaviours they showed as preschoolers, but in secret, and in small groups of friends and siblings. These exploratory games have had different names over the years ('playing doctors', 'mummies and daddies', or just plain 'rudies'), but they all serve the purpose of giving children permission and justification to look at and touch each other's genitals and bottoms. The satisfaction children derive from these games seems to come as much from their intimacy and secrecy as from their sexual nature. In some ways, it is like taking part in a kind of primitive and sacred ritual. Younger children can be brought into these secret games by their siblings, but there is usually no more than one or two years' difference in ages among the children in the group.

How to react

The first step for parents is to accept that a certain amount of displaying, looking at, and touching of genitals is part of normal development. Most parents today are aware of this, and accepting it in principle is not usually a problem. It can be a little more difficult to know how to react when these behaviours actually occur, but the basic principles are simple:
- *Try to stay cool.* Young children can tend to make a game of any behaviours that they know will annoy or upset you, repeating them just to enjoy your reaction.
- *Ignore* minor incidents of flashing, streaking and self-exploration. The more attention you pay to it, the more importance you give it. However, if the behaviour involves touching of yourself or others, then you need to act. Depending on the child's age, either move her hand away without comment and distract her (with toddlers), or stop her and give a brief explanation of why you feel that behaviour is not okay (with preschoolers).
- *Give clear, brief guidelines.* Your explanation of why the behaviour is not okay will depend on your family values and your personal style. You may feel the need to do some hard thinking about the reasons for your discomfort. Avoid using statements like 'That's dirty!' or 'That's disgusting!', which can't possibly help a child to understand why you disapprove of what they are doing. Be clear and specific about which behaviours are okay, which aren't, and why.
- *Use accurate language.* It's much easier to use terms like vagina and penis from the very beginning. The earlier they are introduced into a child's vocabulary, the less chance there is of awkwardness and embarrassment about using them later on. It is also an excellent way of beginning your child's sex education in a simple and natural way. But this doesn't mean that you cannot use more casual and everyday terms. It depends on the

circumstances — the language you use doesn't always have to be anatomically correct.

Sex education

There are now many books available that you can read to and with young children about how their bodies work. This is an excellent way to provide appropriate education in a relaxed and natural setting.

When your child asks questions about her body, or about how babies are made, take the opportunity to provide the basic biological facts in a brief and simple way. As she becomes older, you can obtain books on the subject that she will be able to read for herself.

Take as many opportunities as you can in the early years to provide your children with basic sex education. Even in the most open and enlightened families, it becomes harder to talk about sex when your children reach early adolescence. That's not to say that you shouldn't provide older children with specific information relevant to their stage of development. They will need to know about contraception, sexually transmitted diseases, the risks and implications of beginning sexual activity at an early age, and — most importantly — the ethics and responsibilities of sexuality. Much of this will probably be covered by the health syllabus at your child's secondary school, but your input is still vital, especially in regard to sexual values.

Sexual abuse

Mutual sexual play is a normal part of development for many children, but when does natural curiosity cross the line and become abuse? When does exploration become exploitation? One of the simplest indicators is age difference. As a rough guide, once the age difference between the participating children becomes greater than about eighteen months to two years at the most, there is always the possibility that an older child will coerce or pressure a younger one into activities that the younger child doesn't like.

Natural sexual play between young children is mutual and voluntary. Its character is summed up in the traditional invitation: 'I'll show you mine if you show me yours'. The behaviour is associated with giggly excitement, silliness, and perhaps a delicious sense of naughtiness. If discovered, children will be embarrassed about it rather than fearful or anxious, and may well stop engaging in the behaviour in future if forbidden to do so.

Abusive sexual behaviour (it cannot be called 'play') has a different character. The relationship between the children is no longer one of mutual agreement and voluntary participation. Rather than being a game between same-age friends, the roles are more accurately described as 'perpetrator' and 'victim', with the relationship based on power and coercion. There is likely to be a significant age difference between the participants. The behaviours go beyond simple looking, touching and exploring to definitely sexualised activities including masturbation. Emotions associated with the behaviours are more likely to be anxiety, guilt and fear than giggly silliness or embarrassment.

Making children aware

Knowledge is one of the best defences you can give your child against the possibility of sexual abuse, either by older children or adults. Don't be put off by the worry that talking plainly and openly to your child about the risk of abuse might alarm or frighten her. She will take her cue from you. If you are straightforward and matter-of-fact about it, just as you would be when discussing any other potential danger in her environment, she will accept the message in the same spirit. In your discussion, use plain language, be clear and explicit, and keep it brief. A useful approach is to talk about 'good touching' and 'bad touching' and the differences between the two. Good touching can be described as any form of physical contact that we enjoy and that leaves us feeling comfortable and happy. Bad touching is any kind of physical contact that leaves us feeling uncomfortable or 'yucky'.

Demonstrate what to say and do

Demonstrate to your child what she should say and do if she is ever touched by anyone who makes her feel uncomfortable or scared, and give her some practice in being loud, direct and assertive. Assure her that you will never be angry if she is involved in an incident of bad touching, and that you will always want to know about it.

Your efforts at home will be backed up at school, where 'keeping ourselves safe' is now part of the primary health syllabus.

Keep an eye on them

Your next most important line of defence is to know where your child is at all times. Young children who spend a lot of time in unsupervised play, especially away from home, are at greatly increased risk of abuse. This would seem to be a fairly simple and basic safety rule, yet in my work I continue to see sexually abused young children who have been left free to roam the neighbourhood unsupervised for long periods. These children are obvious targets for older children or adults seeking prey.

In deciding how much freedom and independence to give your child, use your own judgment based on the expert knowledge you have of her. Depending on your child's age, and how sensible and responsible she is, you may not always have to be right on the spot, but keep that parent radar working at all times.

Warning signs of abuse

What are the signs to look out for if you are worried that your child may have been abused? In serious cases of abuse, the warning signs are:
- Obvious physical indications such as bruising, pain, discomfort or infection in the genital or anal area.
- Behavioural changes, which can include withdrawal, or distress without obvious cause.

- An abrupt change in personality.
- A sudden change in sleep pattern.
- Anxiety about being touched or undressed.
- Sexual knowledge and behaviour inappropriate to the child's age.

Bear in mind that none of these signs on its own necessarily indicates abuse, but if you feel you have reasonable grounds for concern, talk to someone with expert knowledge. Your family doctor will be able to advise you whether further action needs to be taken, and if so give you the names of local agencies to contact for assessment and support.

It is difficult even to think about the possibility that our children may have been sexually abused. While you cannot guarantee that it will never happen, you can at least take some decisive steps to reduce the risk to an absolute minimum:

- Be accepting of and knowledgeable about your children's sexual development.
- Create a family climate of open communication in general, and about sexuality in particular.
- Give your children direct instruction and appropriate practice in regard to their sexual safety.
- Be sensibly vigilant about where and with whom your children play.

Parenting points

- Children have a natural sexual awareness from early toddlerhood.
- They move from exploration and awareness of their own bodies to the stage of mutual play.
- Be matter-of-fact and low-key in response to children's sexual behaviour.
- Be as clear as you can in your own mind about your own sexual values.
- Begin your child's sex education at the earliest possible age.
- Protect your child from the risk of sexual abuse by direct, open instruction about their sexual safety.

PART SEVEN
Relationships and communication

17 Television

Televisions have been sitting in the corner of our lounge-rooms for decades now, and no one could doubt the powerful influence they have had on family life during this time.

For as long as television has been around, parents have been worried about the effect it might have on their children's attitudes and behaviour. This has also been a popular topic for research, and a mountain of evidence has piled up over the years on the effects that different types of programmes have on children. Because of the content of many popular programmes, much of the research has looked specifically at whether television violence and aggression can have an impact on children.

Television and violence

Most children watch a lot of television (20-plus hours per week is not uncommon), and many of the most popular programmes contain violence. One United States study showed that 80 per cent of all programmes had some form of violent content, and that this rate had not changed significantly from the 1960s to the 1980s.

Is it possible that children's behaviour can be affected by this? The short answer is yes, but there isn't a simple, direct link between, for example, a child seeing a violent act on television and repeating that act in real life.

Children do learn a great deal of social behaviour by direct imitation of what they see. Before the days of television, they observed the behaviour of their family, friends, and local community. The television screen has vastly increased the range of behavioural models to which children are exposed, from news and documentaries at one extreme, to fantasy adventures and cartoons at the other. But, quite clearly, children do not imitate everything they see on television. They are able to discriminate between fantasy and reality. They may play fantasy games based on television shows, but they understand that they are make-believe. When children *do* change their real-life behaviour or beliefs as a result of something they have seen on television, it is because they perceive it as having relevance to their daily lives, and as something they are actually capable of doing.

So, the risk of children learning inappropriate behaviour from television increases according to how realistic the presentation is, and how close it is to the children's own life situations. After watching a cartoon your child will not race off to drop large rocks from great heights onto passing rabbits or road-runners. But a realistic television presentation of anti-social behaviour by young people, whose age and circumstances are similar to those of your own child, may have some effect.

But even here the link is not direct and simple. Although television does seem to induce a trance-like state in children, it doesn't hypnotise. In other words, seeing an aggressive act on television will not make your child rise like a robot and proceed to carry it out. Quite clearly, the great majority of children can watch violence and aggression on television without any observable effect on their everyday behaviour.

As an indication of how difficult it is to show a direct link between television watching and aggression, although one study found that aggressive children did indeed watch more television than non-aggressive children, and were more interested in violent programmes, it did not establish that watching television *caused* the aggressive behaviour. Perhaps some children are more likely to display aggressive behaviour, regardless of whether or not they watch violent television shows. Or it may be that the children's television viewing habits *matched* their interests and behaviour style, rather than caused them.

Television and the family

For all the above reasons, I have never been greatly worried about the direct effect of television violence on most children's behaviour. Television is only one of the many factors that need to be considered, including influences within the family and the wider community. Of far more concern to me is the effect on family life of the *time* spent watching television.

A family is a group of people who care for each other and spend time with each other. By that I mean not just sitting together watching a flickering picture on a small screen, but talking to each other, sharing the day's experiences, arguing, doing chores together, and sharing enjoyable activities. A family's life, its sense of actually being a family, is created by the interaction of its members. Modern life gives today's families less and less time to be physically together. The seductive lure of television seems to be robbing us of the few precious opportunities that are left in the day simply to enjoy being with the people we love.

Family life also provides innumerable opportunities each day for children to learn new skills and, very importantly, to absorb our values. In addition to the many skills our children learn from us, we also help them to absorb important values, such as sharing, courtesy, respect, and patience.

Most important of all, within their family children learn that they are loved and valued. If not learned there, it may never be. A little girl recently told me that her mother put her to bed 'because Dad is too busy watching his programme'. She then added sadly, 'I don't think he loves me'. Having also spoken to her father I'm pretty sure she wasn't right in her conclusion, but isn't that a sad message for any child to be receiving? A little stab of guilt pricked my own conscience when I thought of the times I have muttered a quick goodnight to my children with one eye on my favourite television show.

Taking control of television

There are some simple and well-known methods to help you minimise the impact that television watching can have on your child.

First, with younger children, monitor and control the programmes they watch. Turn the television on for specific shows rather than for long periods of time. Although it's often very tempting, try not to use television as a babysitter.

Second, with older children, sit down with the television guide and discuss the programmes they would like to watch. Help them to choose suitable shows, and encourage them to switch the set off when those programmes are finished. Help them to be aware of, and limit, their total television viewing time over the course of a week. Make sure that chores, sport and other activities take priority over television.

Third, from time to time sit down and watch some of your children's favourite programmes with them. This will give you the opportunity to keep up with the things that interest them and the chance to talk about the content of the programmes. It will also allow you to check that programmes that sound suitable are in fact appropriate for your child.

Parenting points

- Many children spend significant amounts of their waking lives in front of television, and parents can be rightfully concerned about the effect this can have.
- A major worry for many parents is the possible effect of television violence on their children. As a general rule, the risk of learning inappropriate behaviour from television is increased according to how realistic the presentation is, and how closely it resembles the children's own life situation.
- However, even in this context, some children seem to be more interested in television violence than others, and also more susceptible to its effects.
- Television can rob families of precious time together, and deprive children of real-life learning opportunities.
- There are some simple safeguards that all families can put into place to limit the negative effects of television.

18 Communication

Good communication skills form the foundation of effective parenting. Many of the problems we encounter as parents would be alleviated, or perhaps wouldn't even occur, if we communicated with our children more successfully. Although good communication is important at all ages, the ways in which we communicate with our children will change with each developmental stage.

Communication involves two processes: transmission and reception. The way we talk to our children is important for many reasons, but so too is the way we listen. The ability to listen is a valuable parenting skill from the preschool years upwards, but probably becomes most useful during adolescence (assuming that our children are still talking to us by then!).

Early verbal stimulation

The amount and kind of communication we have with our children during the early years can influence not only their language development, but also their intellectual growth. Babies respond to the sound of their mother's voice even before birth, which shows how sensitive they are to human speech. Verbal stimulation and interaction are vital ingredients in the process by which a young child comes to understand the world and his place in it. In ways that are too complex to discuss here, language is both the stimulus for and foundation of intellectual growth. It is the framework and structure by which we make sense of the world. In the first five years of life, children need to be immersed in a sea of language. Even very young babies will benefit from your running commentary as you go about your business together. Songs, stories, rhymes, questions, statements, descriptions, and explanations all contribute to the richness of a child's verbal environment.

As toddlers begin to develop their own speech, they will take more and more of the initiative in using language, as it becomes an effective tool to help them meet their own needs and understand the objects and events around them. The endless chatter and questions of toddlers and preschoolers can be exhausting, and you will not always have the time or patience to respond, but try to do the best you can. Each question answered can add to your child's understanding of the world.

Communicating instructions

Apart from the importance of a stimulating verbal environment for encouraging your child's intellectual development, there is the more mundane issue of getting them to do what you ask. As children become more mobile and independent, much of what you say to them will take the form of instructions, requests and prohibitions. A few simple rules about these things can save much frustration and wasted breath.

- Get your child's attention before you say something to him. Don't start talking until you know he is listening.
- Make requests or instructions as brief as possible.
- Check that your child has understood you by asking him: 'Okay — now what did I ask you to do?'.
- Don't ask the same thing twenty times before you do something about it. This is guaranteed to produce a very common childhood hearing disorder known as 'parent deafness'. If you ask, be prepared to act.
- Be fair and respectful in your requests.

- Explanations about why you want something done, or not done, are very helpful and important for a child's intellectual and moral development, but tailor them to your child's age level. For maximum effect, regardless of your child's age, short and to the point is best. How many sermons have you dozed through?

Using I-statements

Many writers have stressed the importance of I-statements in expressing feelings, particularly in the context of disagreements. When you have a grievance with your child, it can help to explain how you feel about the situation, and why you feel that way, rather than blaming or abusing him: 'You never ...', 'You always ...', 'You useless ...'. This is because the natural first response to blame and criticism is usually self-defence — if we are attacked, we tend to attack in return. But if someone makes a factual statement about a situation and how he feels about it, there is a greater chance that we will listen to him, think about what he is saying, and perhaps take the message on board. And isn't that the whole point of making a complaint?

When discussing issues or problems with your child, try using the formula: 'I feel ... when you ... because ...'. For example, '*I feel* angry *when you* leave your school bag right by the front door *because* someone might trip over it'. Or perhaps '*I feel* hurt *when you* speak to me like that *because* it is so disrespectful'. Then wait, and give your child a chance to respond.

There is nothing magical about I-statements, but they are more likely to lead to genuine conflict resolution. They allow you to express the strength of and reasons for your feelings in a form that is not hostile or abusive. In the end, wouldn't you prefer your child to change his behaviour because he can see a *reason* for your displeasure, rather than because you can shout more loudly than he can?

Talking with

In day-to-day family life, most of what we say to our children is in the form of requests, commands, directions, or questions. We seldom address comments, observations, or statements about how we feel to our children (other than annoyance perhaps). This is understandable when children are very young, but as they reach late-primary-school age, we can begin to share our feelings and opinions with them.

Telling your child about something that happened to you during the day, or sharing a childhood memory with him, can create an atmosphere of real closeness between you. It can also sometimes help your child to deal with issues of a similar nature that he has been reluctant to tell you about, or give him the confidence to raise a problem with you directly or ask for your advice.

Talking *with* our children gives the message that we respect them enough to share our opinions and feelings with them.

Questions, not nagging

Questions can be a useful alternative to commands and reprimands. Instead of shouting, nagging or lecturing, try asking questions instead, for example:

- Michael is lying on the floor in the lounge-room while his homework sits unopened in his schoolbag.

    Michael, what are you doing?
    Watching television.
    What are you supposed to be doing?
    Er ... homework?
    When do you think you might be able to start?
    As soon as this programme finishes?
    That would be great. Thanks, Michael.

- Rachel is taking her paper and watercolours into the lounge-room to paint on the carpet.

Rachel, where are you going?
I'm going to paint.
Where are you going to paint?
On the floor.
What might happen if you paint on the floor?
(Pauses to think) Some paint might get on the carpet ... or the water might spill?
So where would be a better place to paint?
On the kitchen table.
Good idea.

Questions are more likely to lead to thinking, problem-solving, discussion, and self-initiated behaviour change, provided they are asked in a reasonable way. They are likely to be just as effective as nagging and shouting, with much less possibility of tantrums and tears.

Listening is communication, too

Being a good listener is an important parenting skill, and can bring major benefits to you and your family. By listening actively and attentively to your child you give him the message that you respect and care for him enough to hear what he has to say. Listening is also useful in helping your child to talk about and resolve for himself some of the daily problems with which he has to deal, whether minor or major. And good listening can reduce conflict and argument.

Listening appears to be a simple skill to acquire, but it actually takes a little practice and requires some self-control. This is because the most important part of the listening process — sharing our feelings — doesn't come naturally.

Sharing feelings with children

Family life is based on feelings. Within a family we each try to meet our own needs for love, support, security and a sense of belonging. However, because other family members are sometimes unable to satisfy these needs for us, emotions in families can run high. When these feelings are expressed, our natural response is to react or respond to the content of what is said. For example, children often say things such as:
- You're always picking on me.
- I hate you.
- You're mean.
- How come you never make Jason pick up his toys?

When we hear things like this, our natural tendency as parents is to respond with denial, disbelief, dismissal, or a mountain of evidence to convince the child that he is not just wrong, but seriously deluded. In other words, we usually respond with everything but a simple acceptance of the feeling behind the statement. If your child makes a statement that is obviously strongly felt, it can help to focus on the feeling and acknowledge it:
- You're really feeling pretty angry at me, aren't you?
- You really don't like me right now.
- You don't think I'm being very fair?
- You think I let Jason get away with things?

The effect of doing this can sometimes seem almost miraculous. If your child feels that he is really being listened to, he can let off steam quickly, and the actual problem can then be seen more clearly and objectively. Once the emotional steam has been allowed to escape, the problem often seems to deflate to a manageable size.

If, however, your child's feelings are not heard and acknowledged, frustration will be added to the original problem, leading to further tension and a breakdown in communication.

Active listening

Although 'active' listening, as it is often called, can sometimes be dramatically effective, it takes effort on the part of the listener to do it properly. For example, let's say that your ten-year-old daughter is lying on her bed, obviously grumpy. You ask what the problem is and she says: 'You took David to the supermarket with you after school, and he got a chocolate. You never take me to the supermarket!'.

You now have two choices. You can either try to convince your daughter otherwise by using faultless reasoning, relentless logic, and overwhelming evidence, or you can respond to her grievance with active listening.

The first approach is unlikely to convince her that her complaint is unreasonable, because reason, logic and evidence don't stack up against feelings. It is her *feelings* that must be dealt with before any facts can be looked at; if her feelings are properly addressed, the so-called problem may well disappear.

If you respond to your daughter with active listening, the dialogue might go something like this:

So you're pretty mad with me?
Yeah, I am!
You think it's not fair that I took David to the supermarket without you.
Yeah ... I was really mad when I found out ... I felt left out. Just because he's younger than me, he gets all the good things.
You think he gets good things and you don't.
And he gets away with things because he's little ... he teases me, and if I do anything to him you tell me off and not him.
Sounds to me like there's a few things you're upset about.
Yeah ... if you could realise that just because David's the youngest he shouldn't get away with things. If David and I are having a fight, it's not always my fault.
Okay, I'll try!
(Pause, then quietly) Thanks, Mum.

In this example, the real issue that emerged was fairness. The daughter felt that because her brother was little, he was getting away with things. Her not being taken to the supermarket was really only a minor problem, but it opened the floodgates on a reservoir of resentment which had flowed from her perception that she was being treated unfairly. Trying to address the supermarket incident on its own using reason and persuasion would probably have led only to mutual exasperation.

Active listening in practice

Active listening can be used with all children from preschool age. It involves *identifying* the feeling behind a statement; *focusing on* the feeling; and *following* the feeling as the dialogue proceeds. This is best done by reflecting the feeling that you pick up back to your child, in your own words. For example:

- I hate David!
  You're feeling pretty angry with him?
- Mrs Thomas was really mean to me today.
  Sounds like you're upset about that.
- I don't want to go down to my room in the dark.
  You're feeling a bit scared about it?

At first it will feel awkward and funny to talk like this, but if you concentrate on the feeling your child is trying to express, and do your best to reflect it, it will soon begin to seem more natural.

When your child comes to you with a problem, try not to give advice as your first response every time. Because we don't like to see our children upset, we often try to solve their problem quickly or minimise its importance with band-aid suggestions such as:

- Don't get upset.
- Forget about it.
- You should/shouldn't have ...
- Why didn't you ....?

These kinds of responses are fine sometimes, but they can close down communication at a time when allowing your child to express his feelings about the situation first would eventually lead to a better resolution.

Start with the positive

Rather than beginning with the more difficult emotions of sadness or anger, you might find it helpful to start practising your listening skills with positive feelings, such as happiness, pride and satisfaction:
- Sounds like you had a good day at school today.
- You look pretty happy about the way you played in the second half.
- You seem to be quite pleased with that drawing.

Keep the conversation going with open-ended questions, such as:
- How did you feel when that happened?
- What did you think about that?
- Then what happened?

Practising with positive, non-threatening situations will help you to become comfortable with the technique before trying it in more stressful situations.

Being a good listener can have positive effects on you and your family. It can defuse tensions by allowing your children to express their feelings, rather than keeping them bottled up inside. Listening to your children demonstrates your respect and care for them, and allows you to focus on their world as they are experiencing it. Finally, it is a very useful way of helping children to deal with the negative feelings that result from life's painful experiences, whether minor or major.

Communication and family meetings

Many parenting writers have described the importance of regular family meetings to discuss, plan, and problem-solve. In fact, family meetings bring together all the communication skills we have been talking about. They provide the opportunity for discussion on problem issues, for problem-solving based on reason rather than the use of power, and for the use of good listening skills. They also reassure children that their views on family matters are valued and respected. Research has shown that a democratically run family — in which there is respect for the rules, respect for the rights of the individual, and lots of discussion — is associated with better emotional adjustment and greater self-esteem in children. Family meetings are democracy in action.

Parenting points

- Good communication skills form the basis of effective parenting.
- Language is both a stimulus for and the foundation of intellectual growth.
- Make sure that you have your child's attention before you speak to him.
- Keep requests or instructions brief and to the point.
- Repeating yourself many times before you act is guaranteed to produce 'parent deafness' in children.
- I-statements are a useful way to express your feelings. Use the formula: 'I feel ... when you ... because ...'.
- Remember to talk *with* your child sometimes, rather than *at* him.
- Asking questions can be a useful way to manage behaviour without nagging.
- To be a good listener, you need to focus on the *feelings* behind what your child is saying.
- Family meetings are the ideal context in which to practise effective communication techniques.

19 When parents separate

For an increasing number of couples, the dreams, hopes and happiness of marriage end in grief, anger and bitterness. Regrettably, the torrent of hurtful and destructive emotions that can be released by divorce can also engulf children. How does separation and divorce affect children, and what can parents do in such situations to protect their children from emotional damage?

Children first

Good parenting is hard work. It involves a daily list of tasks and responsibilities that we need to fulfil in order to meet our children's needs. This often means that parents have to put their own needs to one side, and coping with the effects of divorce presents one of the biggest challenges that any parents can face. Right when two people have to adjust to the shock and pain of the destruction and disappearance of a major part of their lives, they also have to put their own feelings on hold in order to minimise damage to their children. Somehow, from somewhere, has to come the courage and selflessness to submerge the grief and hurt in order to protect the emotional survival of their children. At a time when their feelings can be almost overwhelming, and when their partner may be the last person they want to talk to, parents have to be able to discuss and plan for meeting the children's needs first.

Effects on children

Divorce can have a major and long-lasting effect on children's lives. This is because it often occurs at a time when they are totally dependent on their parents for their physical and emotional survival. One of the greatest fears of childhood is that of abandonment. Combine this with the pain and aching grief that goes along with the possible loss of a loved parent, and it is easy to see why the impact on children can be so great. Parents are the foundation of a child's life, and divorce can shake that foundation like an earthquake.

Each child and each family situation is unique, so it is not possible to predict exactly what will happen to any particular child. The chances are, however, that children will experience some or all of the emotions of sadness, fear, anxiety, anger and guilt.

Discovering that their parents are going to live apart will almost certainly make children very sad, except perhaps in cases where one parent has been abusive and violent. They will be tearful and may become very quiet and withdrawn. They will probably worry that if one parent can leave, maybe the other will as well, and so might become very clingy and dependent. They may have nightmares or refuse to sleep in their own beds. They will probably worry about how the non-custodial parent is managing on his or her own, and feel sad for them. Preschoolers may regress in their behaviour, perhaps starting to soil or wet again.

Children who are feeling hurt, confused, and helpless because of the separation of their parents sometimes express their frustration through tantrums and defiance. They may feel that one or other parent is to blame for what has happened, and show their anger through hostile words and behaviour.

It is also common for children to experience a sense of guilt as if somehow they have caused the separation. They will often be anxious that something they have done has caused one parent to leave the home, and may ask: 'Was it because I was naughty?'.

Some of these negative emotional effects can be worsened over time because of the additional burdens faced by the custodial parent. He or she may have to cope with shifting house, surviving on a reduced income, dealing with grief and loneliness, and having to be two parents in one. Even though the end of an unhappy marriage can bring relief, the first few years following separation and divorce can be worse than the last years of the relationship.

What can you do?

Even though it can seem almost impossible during the emotional tornado of a separation, parents' main task is to try to separate their relationship with their partner from their role as parents.

When their parents separate, children need:
- to be protected from adult conflict and argument;
- to know what is going to happen; and
- to have contact with both parents.

First, children need to be shielded from the distress and anxiety caused by seeing and hearing their parents argue. The evidence of research shows that there is only one thing worse for children's adjustment than a fighting marriage, and that is a fighting divorce.

Second, children need to be told about the separation before it occurs. They need to be told, in simple, non-blaming terms, why it is happening. They need to know who they will be living with, where they will be living, and how often they will be seeing the non-custodial parent. They need to be reassured repeatedly that they are in no way to blame for the separation, that both parents still love them very much and will never stop being their parents, even though they might not live together.

Third, children need to spend as much time as possible with both parents. Research indicates that children who make the best adjustment to divorce maintain frequent contact with the non-custodial parent. Unfortunately, some parents carry on their marriage wars after their divorce, and use their children as the weapons. For example, some parents try to make it as difficult as possible for the other parent to see the children, and try to enlist the children as allies against their former partner. This is extremely destructive and damaging to the children. It places them in a distressing, unwinnable conflict of loyalties. Children usually work hard to be fair to both parents, want to have contact with both, and don't want to hurt either of them. Knowing that one parent is hostile to the other makes an already difficult situation even harder for them to handle. The exception to the rule that frequent contact with the non-custodial parent is beneficial for children is when such contact means frequent opportunities for conflict. If either party uses access visits as occasions to criticise or undermine the other parent, the children will undoubtedly become distressed and confused. In these circumstances, one or other parent should initiate couple counselling to ensure that access remains beneficial rather than harmful.

Finally, both parents should try to ensure that access arrangements are observed faithfully and reliably. I have heard many sad stories of the heartache and disappointment that children experience when parents postpone or cancel an access visit, or, even worse, simply fail to turn up. If, as a non-custodial parent, you are not able or prepared to regard your visitation responsibilities as sacrosanct, it may be better for you to decide to take no further part in your child's development. This at least gives children a chance to rebuild their lives on the basis of some predictability and consistency, rather than being continually hurt by disappointment and uncertainty.

Communication after separation

The inescapable fact about separation is that it is not an isolated event, but an ongoing process. Your former partner is not going to disappear off the face of the earth (no matter what you might wish). If you have children you will simply have to continue communication on a multitude of issues, from missing socks to major decisions about schooling and health. In the children's interests, this communication needs at least to be polite. The one factor that will give your children the best chance of successful adjustment after separation is your ability to talk to your partner in a civilised way.

Children's feelings

To help your children through the emotional aftermath of separation, you will need to practise your active-listening skills (see Chapter 18). You need to let your children express their feelings of hurt, sadness, anxiety and anger. Let these emotions flow, even though it may be distressing for you to hear them. Nothing can fix the pain for children in the short term, but allowing them to express their feelings can help children accept and adjust to it a little more easily.

There are many books and stories written for children of all ages on the subject of separation and divorce, and they can be useful in helping children get in touch with their emotions, understand more about what is happening to them, and give them the hope that things will get better. Ask at your local library.

The long-term outcome

There is no doubt that divorce hurts children. There is also no doubt that parents' behaviour at the time of separation and afterwards can moderate its harmful effects. Much research over the last 30 years has shown that the majority of children can survive their parents' separation with no obvious emotional scars and without a significant impact on their day-to-day functioning. Within two to three years, there is a good chance that they will have adjusted to their changed circumstances and lifestyle. But almost all these children will continue to wish that their parents had never separated, and will cherish the unrealistic fantasy that one day they will reunite.

Long-term research also shows that despite superficial adjustment, the children of divorced parents can have significant problems with the success and stability of their own relationships as adults.

Although there is evidence that separation is better for children than a conflict-ridden marriage, the effects, consequences and implications of marriage breakdown tend to remain with children for life.

Parenting points

- Separation presents parents with the challenge of putting their children's needs first at a time when their own emotional survival is under threat.
- Parental separation causes children to feel sadness, fear, anxiety, anger and guilt.
- Parents have to cope with these negative emotional effects on their children at a time when their own life circumstances have been drastically altered.
- Above all, children need to be protected as much as possible from adult conflict and arguments.
- Children need to be reassured as often as necessary that the separation was not their fault.
- Children need the security of knowing, as far as possible under the circumstances, exactly what is going to happen to them.
- They need as much contact as possible with both parents, provided that contact does not mean conflict.
- Civilised communication between parents will go a long way towards minimising the destructive emotional impact of separation, and helping children adjust to their new circumstances.
- In the long term most children make a good superficial adjustment to their parents' separation, but the effects will remain with them, in one way or another, for life.
- For the sake of the children it is vital at the time of separation that parents do their best to separate their relationship with their ex-partner from their role as a parent.

20 Self-esteem

One of our important tasks as parents is to send our children out into the world with a strong and healthy sense of self-esteem. Self-esteem has a decisive influence on our ability to function as effective, independent, emotionally stable individuals. Our approach to life can vary from confident, positive, and optimistic, to hesitant, negative, and pessimistic, depending on our sense of self-worth.

Whatever talents and potential a child is born with may come to nothing unless activated and given direction by a sense of self-esteem. Low self-esteem can not only sap a child's natural optimism and zest for living, but in the worst cases it can convert these positive forces into a harmful energy directed both at self and society.

What is self-esteem?

Self-esteem is another way of referring to a person's positive or negative self-concept. If someone feels generally okay about himself, and can give himself a good overall passing grade as a person, he is said to have a positive self-concept, a good self-image, or high self-esteem. If someone gives himself an overall failing grade as a person, he would be described as having a negative self-concept, a poor or negative self-image, low self-esteem, or lack of self-worth.

Self-concept is a kind of jigsaw puzzle put together from all those physical, psychological, and behavioural characteristics that make us the individuals we are. Each piece in the puzzle is a different aspect of ourselves — the things we like to do, what we are good at, the things that worry us, our history of happy or unhappy experiences, of success and failure, our perception of how we perform in different situations, our ideals, and our physical appearance. This complex, multi-faceted picture of ourselves is our self-concept.

We also tend to evaluate each of the components that make up our self-concept. That is, we can have either positive or negative feelings about how we get on with others, our performance at work or school, whether we are living up to our goals, and so on. Most of us tend to judge ourselves continually against the standards of what we would like to be, or feel that we should be. Imagine each piece of the self-concept jigsaw puzzle as having a plus or minus sign on it, according to how we evaluate that particular aspect of ourself. If the sum of all these positive and negative signs is definitely on the credit side, our overall self-concept is likely to be positive. If the balance tips more towards the debit side, so will our self-concept.

Signs of high self-esteem

Young people with high self-esteem have a positive, optimistic and energetic approach to life. They have a sense of trust in their own competence and are willing to try new experiences. They have a realistic awareness and acceptance of their strengths and relative weaknesses, and an ability to evaluate their own performance objectively. They are able to accept criticism without defensiveness or hostility, and can tolerate failure without giving up. They value and respect themselves as individuals, and have an accepting, friendly, respectful attitude towards others.

In contrast, children with low self-esteem tend to have a negative, pessimistic approach to life. They lack confidence in themselves, and are reluctant to try new experiences. They have difficulty evaluating their strengths and weaknesses objectively, and have a strong need for reassurance and praise from others. They find it hard to accept criticism without defensiveness or hostility, and tend to overreact to failure. They may see themselves as helpless, powerless, and ineffective. Their attitude towards others may be negative, mistrustful, or hostile.

How to develop self-esteem

Self-esteem is created by a person's life experiences and begins to be shaped from the earliest years. Parents play a major role in that shaping process. Fortunately, the basic ingredients in nurturing children's self-esteem come instinctively to parents, although it may require a little effort to use them consistently.

Unconditional love

The first and most indispensible ingredient is love. For children to develop a sense of self-esteem, they need to feel that they are loved. Self-esteem is based on love in the same way that a house is built on a foundation — an unstable foundation means a shaky house. Children are unlikely to develop a secure sense of self-worth unless they are loved unconditionally. Children who do not experience the security of a loving relationship with their parents from the earliest years may develop an attitude of anxious self-doubt, rather than one of basic trust in their own worth and abilities.

We express love for our children through physical affection, words, and by providing for their needs. They don't need to be swamped with caresses and affection, or to be made the centre of our world. We need only to assure them through what we do and say that they are cared for and valued.

It is also important, as has been said many times, to distinguish between the *child* and his *behaviour*. Reassure your child that even though you may sometimes growl at him and punish him for what he has done, it is his behaviour that annoys you. Being angry with him doesn't mean you don't love him.

Respect for children

Respect is an important ingredient of genuine love. If we truly love and care for our children, there will always be an element of respect in the way we respond to them. This involves being able to see past the fact that they are our own children, and being aware of their uniqueness and rights as developing individuals.

At a minimal level, we demonstrate respect for our children by providing for their basic physical needs, protecting them from danger and illness, and not subjecting them to any form of deliberate abuse, whether physical or mental. Ideally, of course, respecting children means more than just acknowledging their rights to have their basic needs met. It means recognising them as young people with their own personalities and potential. In the hurly-burly of family life it is easy to overlook the fact that children are developing human beings who happen to be under our guardianship. As their guardians, it is our role and responsibility to protect and nurture their uniqueness.

We can show respect for children in the way we communicate with them — by really listening to them, and by talking *with* them rather than *at* them (see Chapter 18). We also need to think about how we speak to our children. We can convey messages of respect through simple, daily acts of politeness, such as a friendly greeting, the use of 'please' and 'thank you', apologising when we are in the wrong, and asking permission before we use things belonging to them.

Respect and trust go hand in hand. We show our respect for our children by trusting them to do the right thing, to be responsible, and by believing in their inborn desire to become independent and self-sufficient. By doing this, we actually increase the chances that they will behave independently and responsibly, because children tend to behave as we expect them to. When children are learning a new skill, try to give them as much instruction and encouragement as you can, but also try to trust in their ability to do the rest for themselves. When we trust our children to do the right thing, and show our confidence in them, we provide the circumstances for them to grow to their potential with a strong and healthy sense of their own abilities and worth.

Finally, each child is an individual with a unique personality, and a unique profile of skills and abilities. Every child has a pattern of strengths and weaknesses that is theirs alone. We need to be aware of that pattern, to encourage the development of potential strengths, and to accept that our children may always find some skills difficult to achieve. If we know and respect our children's individuality, and give them the opportunity and encouragement to develop whatever talents they may have, we will inevitably help the growth of their self-esteem.

Encouraging independence

Our bottom-line responsibility as parents is to our prepare children for ultimate independence. We have done our job properly when children leave the nest as well-adjusted, confident young adults prepared to establish their own lives.

Independence and self-esteem are closely related. As children conquer the challenges that life presents, they see themselves more positively. As they learn new skills they become more confident and less dependent on others, which increases their sense of self-worth.

Children have a natural and strong desire to do things for themselves. So, all we have to do is foster and encourage that desire, giving them the opportunities and support they need. Just look at the determination of a baby learning to reach out, roll over, crawl, and walk. His parents need to be there to look after his safety, but the drive to do these things comes from within.

In today's busy families, there is always the temptation to do things for children that they could easily do for themselves. We need to be realistic, of course, and accept that as we rush to meet all the deadlines of family life, not every task can be turned into an opportunity for a child to learn a new skill. On the other hand, children must be given the chance to become independent. Children's self-worth is related to the degree of control they feel they have over their own lives. If we can encourage and support our children's attempts to be self-reliant in the daily activities of life — from dressing and feeding in the early years, to making responsible choices as teenagers — children will begin to see themselves as competent individuals.

The old belief that our character is shaped by the way we respond to difficulties is still valid and relevant today. If we want our children to respond positively to challenges, we should expose them gradually to a widening range of new tasks to be mastered. As a child's competence grows, so will his self-confidence.

A sense of belonging

Human beings are social creatures. It is important for our psychological health that we belong to groups in which we feel valued as individuals. Being isolated is normally experienced as unpleasant and undesirable. We can enhance our sense of well-being, and our self-concept, by belonging to and identifying with certain groups.

For most of us, our basic sense of belonging and security comes from being part of a family. Its size can vary from the nuclear family of many western societies to the large extended family characteristic of many other cultures. Whatever their cultural background, most families value contact with their kin. The benefits of this contact are obvious to anyone who has ever seen children enjoying one another's company at a family gathering. In addition, being part of such a gathering gives children a real sense of their wider identity, of how they fit into a network of people who value them, and in which they play a small but important part. Teaching children about family history can help to strengthen their sense of identity, of being a link in a chain that goes back many generations and that will continue for generations to come. It can give them a comforting sense of security and belonging, and adds a further dimension to their self-concept.

There are many other organisations to which children can belong that will give them a sense of identity, such as schools, sports teams, and youth or church groups. Not only can children feel a sense of pride from belonging to such groups, but their self-esteem can be boosted as they acquire the new skills that the group teaches and expects them to perform.

In teams of various sorts, there can be the extra satisfaction of the child knowing that when the team is successful, he has played a part in achieving that success. This kind of satisfaction has a special quality because it combines the pleasure of doing a job well with a sense of comradeship and belonging.

What happens in families probably has the greatest impact on children's basic self-esteem, but membership of other groups can develop important aspects of how they see themselves. It can help children to recognise who they are, what they can do well, their place in the world, and the important contribution they can make to the goals of a group. Family and other groups all have the potential to give children a sense of identity, worth and purpose.

Praising and encouraging

There is no doubt that praise is food for children's self-esteem. Even just a few words of recognition for achievement or effort can have a profound influence on a child's perception of himself, and on his sense of well-being. Children need praise to:
- feel good about themselves;
- motivate and encourage them during new learning experiences;
- develop a sense of competence; and
- become aware of their strengths.

As they attempt new tasks and develop new skills, children need positive feedback from the adults around them. Recognition of effort and improvement helps to motivate them when the going gets a little tough, and to feel good about themselves as a result. Each new success adds to a growing feeling of confidence, and to their perception of themselves as capable and competent. Praise provides the psychological fuel to keep the whole process moving along.

In the day-to-day struggle of parenthood it's easy to fall into the trap of focusing on the negative, and of commenting only when things haven't been done, or haven't been done correctly. We sometimes need to make a conscious effort to look for the good things our children are doing, and to acknowledge them. If you think that you may have fallen into a rut of negativity with your child, you can lift yourself out of it with the 'once-a-day' rule — find one thing every day, however small, that you can acknowledge, compliment, or appreciate.

In my book *Confident Children* (OUP, 1994) I provide specific guidelines for parents who wish to nurture their children's self-esteem to help them develop a confident, positive approach to life.

Parenting points

To develop a healthy sense of self-esteem in your children:
- Make sure they feel loved for who they are, with no strings attached.
- Express your affection verbally, physically, and often.
- Respect their dignity and rights as unique human beings.
- Listen to them and talk *with* them, not *at* them.
- Encourage independence and support them when they are learning new skills.
- Trust them, and have confidence in their competence.
- Acknowledge effort and achievement with praise whenever you can.

Where to go for help

For many of the problems discussed in this book you will need professional guidance and support. Where can you go for help?

Your family doctor

Your family doctor is an ideal first stop to discuss any parenting worries you may have. Some doctors have a particular interest in children's health and family issues, and may be able to advise you directly. If not, your doctor will certainly know the most appropriate local agency or professional to refer you to. Possibilities include paediatricians, family therapists, child psychiatrists, child psychologists, or child-health clinics. Community nurses who work with mothers, babies and young children can also provide useful advice and support for families.

Paediatricians

A paediatrician is a doctor who specialises in children's health. Your family doctor may refer you to one for assessment of issues such as delayed development, toileting difficulties, bedwetting, and ADHD. Some paediatricians take a broader perspective than just medically based problems and may also offer advice on behavioural and learning difficulties.

Family therapists

Family therapists are counsellors who focus on children's behavioural problems within the context of the family. They tend to take the presenting problem as a starting point for looking at family dynamics, that is the relationships and interactions between all family members. The presenting difficulty may be seen as an expression of the way in which a family works, rather than as a problem that resides within the child. Family therapists work from a wide variety of theoretical backgrounds too numerous to describe here.

Child psychiatrists

Child psychiatrists are doctors who specialise in the area of child and adolescent mental health. They deal with serious disorders of thought and mood, such as depression, anxiety, obsessive-compulsive disorder, and schizophrenia, and are able to prescribe medication for these problems. They may also work with other behavioural difficulties such as ADHD, autism, and acting-out teenagers. Some child psychiatrists are hospital-based, while others work in private practice.

Child psychologists

Child psychologists are not medical doctors, although they may have a degree (PhD) that gives them the title of 'Doctor'. They have been trained in psychology and child development, and specialise in dealing with children's behavioural problems. Psychologists have different emphases in their approach to working with children and families, but most tend to deal with the presenting problems in a practical, behavioural way. Some child psychologists are hospital-based, some work in schools, and others are in private practice.

Child and family clinics

Most hospitals have free, multi-disciplinary child and family clinics that combine the services of a wide range of child-health professionals. These can include paediatricians, child psychiatrists, nurses, child psychologists, occupational therapists, and speech therapists.

Family-counselling agencies

A wide variety of churches and community agencies provide free or variable-fee counselling services for children and families. The counsellors in these agencies come from a range of training backgrounds.

Regardless of where you go for support, don't be afraid to ask about qualifications, experience, theoretical approach, and fees before you arrange an appointment.

Index

abilities *see* talent
accelerated learning *see* hot-housing
ADD/ADHD 95–110
  at school 105–7
  diagnosis of 100
  differences between 97–8
  features of 97–9
  medication for 108–9
  in preschool years 100–3
aggression 76–8
anger management
  for children 78–80
  for parents 73
attachment *see* bonding
Azrin, Mathan 22

bedwetting 43–54
  bladder training 47–8, 51–2
  causes of 43–5
  medication 48
  treatment for 45–53
  urine alarm 47, 52–3
bonding 4–7
brain growth 10
Brazelton, Dr T. Berry 92

communication 138–47
  and family meetings 147
  early 138–9
  listening as 142, 144–6
  of feelings 143
  of instructions 139–40

developmental checklists 16
Douglas, Jo
Down's syndrome 16
dyslexia *see* specific learning disability

early intervention 15–17
enuresis *see* bedwetting

family meetings 147

gender 120–3
gifted children 12–13
Green, Dr Christopher 30–1

heredity 90–3
hot-housing 9–14
hyperactivity *see* ADD/ADHD

ignoring 61–2, 66
instructions 139–140
I-statements 140

language development 10–12, 138–9
LD *see* specific learning disability
listening 142–3, 146

active 144–6
love *see* bonding

MacDonald, Kathy 39–30

Neonatal Behavioural Assessment Scale (NBAS) 92–3
night terrors 37–8

night waking 26–34
  in babies 26–33
  in older children 33
nightmares 37–41
  treatment 39–41

personality 91–4
punishment 72

reading 11, 116–17
reasoning 59
Richman, Naomi 31
rules 58–9, 72

Scharf, Martin 53
Sears, Dr William 28
self-esteem 154–61
  definition 154–5
  high 155
  low 155–6
  how to develop 156–61
self-talk
  and ADHD 106
  and anger 79
separation 148–53
  and children's needs 150–1
  effects on children 149–50
sexual behaviour 124–31
  in preschoolers 126
  in school-age children 126–7
  in toddlers 124–5
sex education 127–8
sex roles *see* gender
sexual abuse 128–31
  signs of 130–1
sexual behaviour 124–31
sibling rivalry 82–8
  and new baby 82–6
  between older children 86–8
sleep cycles 36
sleep patterns 27
sleepwalking 41–2
smacking 69–74
  avoidance of 71–3
  effectiveness of 70–1
soiling 23–4
specific learning disability 111–18
  and ADHD 113
  assessment of 113
  causes of 113
  features of 112
  how to help 114, 117–18

talent 12–13, 93
tantrums 62
television 113–7
  and aggression 133–4
  and family life 135–7
  taking control of 136–7
temperament 92–3
time-out 65–8
  duration of 67–8
  location of 67
  procedure 66–7
toddlers 56–63
toilet training 19–24